The
ART
of
BUSINESS
SEDUCTION

The

ART

of

BUSINESS
SEDUCTION

A 30-Day Plan
to Get Noticed,
Get Promoted,
and Get Ahead

MARK JEFFRIES

WILEY

John Wiley & Sons, Inc.

ISBN 978-0-470-59618-0 (cloth)
ISBN 978-0-470-64304-4 (ebk)
ISBN 978-0-470-64305-1 (ebk)
ISBN 978-0-470-64306-8 (ebk)

Printed in the United States of America.

10 9 8 7 6 5 4 3 2 1

CONTENTS

ACKNOWLEDGMENTS

First—Advice For Living—a smart and sharp team constantly introducing ideas, challenge, and humor and always keeping me on my toes.

Dan Ambrosio for spotting the potential of the title and trusting us to deliver a book worthy of the Wiley Publishing Empire!

My fabulous kids, Ollie and Hannah, who add so much comedy, love, and endless examples of core communication.

My beautiful wife, Karen, who is always there for me with so much love and support.

And my wonderful clients, who trust me to stand up in front of their people and customers at events all over the world—an experience that keeps me learning, motivated, and brimming with new concepts.

The
ART
of
BUSINESS
SEDUCTION

INTRODUCTION

"Mrs. Robinson, you're trying to seduce me."

In this famous scene from the movie *The Graduate,* Dustin Hoffman's character knows all too well the power of seduction—yet he stands there unable to resist. As in that iconic scene, seduction commonly refers to romantically luring another into the bedroom.

But in a much broader sense, seduction can simply be about winning over other people, attracting them, and enticing them.

We all have a memory of being seduced by the charms of another. From grade school until now it is hard to resist someone who knows the exact right things to say and do.

I now know these things. And I will teach them to you.

Imagine having that same power in a business setting. A world where your boss, clients, and co-workers all admire you, respect you, and are desperate to be around you and help you get what you want.

There is no more powerful information you need to put to use in your career. By reading my book and educating yourself in the Art of Business Seduction you will own that power and put it to use to get you exactly what you want.

In today's ultracompetitive business environment, it's imperative that you have enough firepower in your arsenal to come out ahead in any situation—especially in business. Understanding the powers of seduction will give you the edge you need. Whether it's persuading a ticketing agent to bump you up to first class on a cross-country flight when traveling to the other coast to meet clients, negotiating a greater salary increase during your annual review, talking the hostess at the hottest restaurant in town into giving you the corner table when you don't have a reservation, or scoring a date with the best-looking man or woman in the room even though that person is clearly out of your league, if you've had any luck under any such circumstances, it's undoubtedly because you were able to use your charms to seduce an unsuspecting party. But if you've been stonewalled by the ticket agent, your boss, the hostess, or even worse, the attractive man or woman, then your powers of seduction need some fine-tuning; or perhaps need to be brought to life. Don't be alarmed. This isn't a case of being unable to teach an old dog new tricks—fortunately, anyone can master the art of seduction.

The key to being a successful seducer is understanding your target audience and giving them exactly what they want. If this sounds insincere, it's not meant to be. Yes, seduction is part performance but this does not mean your actions should not be genuine. As far as I'm concerned, performance simply means demonstrating behavior that's appropriate for a specific situation—and if this behavior results in a pay raise, job or contract, or indeed an upgrade, a reservation, or a date, you tell me what's wrong with that. After all, isn't the goal of any business (or social) interaction to get what you want; and better yet, get what you deserve?

Still, most people do not appreciate that seduction can be a valuable tool in helping them achieve success in business.

However, you are going to need more than a bit of charm and a wide-eyed and open-minded philosophy to master business seduction. You must be willing to change your behavior and your attitude while undergoing the 30-day success makeover this book prescribes. By following the lessons in this book, you will become a master of seduction in just 30 days. It's a generally accepted scientific fact that if you incorporate behavioral changes into your life for 30 consecutive days, then these changes will become inculcated into your lifestyle and in turn become part of your routine. Day by day and week by week, this book will map out a game plan for making you a master of seduction. This book is both a practical guide to achieving success and a blueprint to living the life of your dreams.

This 30-day program will help you develop a sixth sense. (No, you won't see dead people!) You will see things before they start to happen—allowing you to think quickly on your feet and react accordingly. You will not only become a master of seduction, but you will also become a master of playing hunches. More to the point, you'll learn to trust your gut more and more. Just as an experienced parent knows his or her child is sick before the first symptoms appear, or a longtime driving instructor anticipates his student is about to hit the curb when trying to parallel park, or a poker pro knows when to fold his hand even though he is holding a pair of Aces, as soon as you learn the lessons of business seduction you'll become adept at playing your hunches. Upon joining a business crowd in a social situation, you'll be able to immediately read and assess the dynamics of what's going on and your newly honed instincts will kick in, enabling you to begin the process of seducing your target.

In the book *Outliers,* author Malcolm Gladwell determined that if you practice a certain craft (playing violin or chess, for example) for more than 10,000 hours during the course of your lifetime, you will become a world-class expert. The beauty of this book is that it will make you a world-class expert at business seduction in much less time than 10,000 hours. Upon committing to the L-WAR program, you will learn to process information in a different light. You will soon come to understand the valuable insights you can garner from the sound of someone's voice or the way he makes eye contact or shakes your hand upon introduction or from the clothes on his back. Bits of data like these might seem insignificant if viewed on their own, but when looked at as parts of a whole, they are like chapters in a novel, with each helping tell a richer and more truthful story. Think of these details as clues, and like a detective when you piece them all together, you'll see how they will help reveal how an individual is truly feeling and provide you with the opportunity to tailor how you act for this specific interaction. As you go through the 30-day behavior modification process, I promise you'll become so adept at reading and understanding others that all guesswork will vanish from the equation and soon you'll immediately be able to make spot-on and split-second judgments on how to attack any situation. There will no longer be pausing on your end or time for consideration. You'll confidently let your newly honed instincts lead the way to success.

Presently, the world of business is a tumultuous and scary mess; and succeeding in business has never been more difficult. Many believe that this economic climate rivals that of the Great Depression and I appreciate that it can be a difficult choice to concentrate on seducing when so many people are simply concentrating on surviving. That's why today, more than ever, you need an edge—something that gives you a leg up on the competition. My 30-day makeover will give you just that edge. Massive layoffs have left fewer jobs available and an incredibly deep talent pool competing for those limited opportunities. It's a buyer's market, and employers are fully aware of this fact. Sometimes, the only way to beat the competition is to impress the person interviewing you in the first few seconds of your meeting before your resume becomes the center of the conversation and experience and qualifications ever come in to play. This is just one example in which business seduction can and will set you apart. And once you get the job, keeping the job is your next battle. It's no secret; you have to sell yourself every day. The lessons you'll learn from this book will train you how to get noticed for the right reasons by the right people. But even if you're not in business, the beauty of this book is that it lends itself to all aspects of your life. From romantic relationships to family squabbles to social encounters, this book shows you how to navigate through the most difficult and awkward situations. Whether it's business or pleasure, if it involves interacting with other individuals, you need to commit to learning the lessons in this book so that you always get your message across in the most convincing manner possible.

The art of business seduction frees you to effortlessly connect with and influence others so that they not only come to believe they want you and the services you offer, but even more impressive, they'll believe they need you for their own success. Let's be honest, everybody wants something. And the path to success lies in delivering to a variety of people under a variety of circumstances what it is they want. At the same time, and without them being any the wiser, business seduction allows you to convince these people that you are the person they want to hire or the person they want to do business with, and once they come to this realization, they believe all their problems will be solved.

Easier said than done, you are probably thinking. Well, the good news is, anyone can become a master of business seduction. All you need to do is implement my surefire four-step process—L-WAR (Listen, Watch, Anticipate, React)—for 30 days while also concentrating on fine-tuning your strategic communication and soft skills. If you're shaking your head in confusion, let me first explain L-WAR step by step.

Step 1. Listen: It's not about what you have to say; rather, it's about using what the other person has to say in order to get what you want. Listening is not just hearing the words that come out of someone's mouth; listening is also being able to understand what those words mean. It's essential that when listening, you also take time to consider whether what someone says is actually code for something else. So, to be a great listener you also need to be an astute interpreter. For example: Your wife says *I wish the kitchen weren't such a mess.* This sounds like a simple declarative statement. But what your wife is really saying is, "Please clean up the kitchen for me." Listen to what people have to say, but more importantly, listen to what they mean.

Step 2. Watch: Your audience can say whatever they like with their mouths; but their unspoken language—what they say with their eyes, hands, and bodies—will provide you with a wealth of valuable knowledge. Unfortunately, this kind of feedback slips past most other people. If the person you are speaking with blinks a lot, she is likely nervous; if her eyes go up before answering a question, it indicates a lack of knowledge; and if her eyes look down before speaking, it can indicate someone who is lying or feels unworthy of the interaction. When it comes to your audience, their actions speak louder than their words—so watch and learn.

Step 3. Anticipate: Being able to foresee a problem or challenge before it presents itself is the sign of a sharp thinker and a person who can be trusted to help work through a challenge. Familiarity with a subject, process, or company helps you anticipate problems that might arise and offer quick-thinking solutions that can save the day. In learning how to skillfully anticipate, one helpful hint is to try putting yourself in someone else's shoes and seeing the world through his eyes. Ask yourself what would you want to hear or how would you like to be treated, if your roles were reversed? This different perspective will alter and broaden your approach when communicating with this person and allow you to see things more clearly and stay ahead of the curve.

Step 4. React: This is the culmination of the three previous steps and proof that you not only recognize what someone wants, but can give it to her. In a meeting, if you see your audience sit forward, keep going—they like what they are hearing. If they lean back, change course—they have lost interest. Nodding regularly might *not* mean they agree, but rather that they are simply happy for you to go on. If they keep checking their wristwatch, make your point and wrap it up. Time is important to these people and they have other meetings and business they need to tend to. By being aware of these subtle clues that often go unrecognized, you'll change the course of your relationship with this person so that you always have the upper hand.

When you decide to undertake this success makeover, think of yourself as a state-of-the-art computer monitoring every aspect of someone's communication process. You will no longer just listen to what someone says, but you will watch, read, interpret, contextualize, and then adapt and react to what the situation calls for. You should be constantly asking yourself as you observe other people: *If I was that person, what would I want to see and hear?* As the 30 days unfold, your eyes will become open to a world of communication that had more than likely previously gone unnoticed. But using this new wealth of information will allow you to seduce your target audience into both wanting to do business with you, and their believing they need you to be in business with them. By following the L-WAR mandate you'll become an expert at decision making. When you correctly deploy the lessons and techniques found in this book, your mind will begin to think in a certain way and upon each and every encounter, whether business or pleasure, you'll process all the available information, follow your hunches and instincts, and then act accordingly every time. And the beauty of the program is that you won't have to invest the 10,000 hours Malcolm Gladwell suggests to become an expert—you'll see the results in just 30 days (which is less than 1,000 hours!).

Think of the four steps (L-WAR) as the engines of your success. These engines need fuel, and this is where soft skills come in. *Soft skills* are strategic communication techniques that complement your hard skills—which are specific abilities and qualifications that allow you to practice your profession. For a software developer, a *hard skill* is the ability to write code; for an accountant, it's an aptitude for numbers; and for a lawyer, it's the knowledge of law and the ability to argue a case. If you think of your life as a meal, hard skills are the meat and potatoes. Soft skills, on the other hand, are the sauce that enriches what's on the plate by adding a variety of flavors, spice, and sweetness—the otherwise key component in turning an ordinary meal into an extraordinary dining experience.

Soft skills energize business seduction and can be applied to the way you dress and your personal style. Soft skills consist of everything from how you enter a room to how you shake hands. It's networking, but much more than collecting business cards or connecting to others on LinkedIn. Most important, soft skills help introduce your promise and potential that help elevate you above the crowd. Effectively implementing this variety of soft skills allows you to control what you have to offer, and more importantly, how others perceive you. Every scenario allows for a different variety of seduction.

In front of a CEO, you'll want to appear confident, competent, and in control. In front of a new client, you are inspirational and motivating—helping them visualize how you can help.

Remember: Your confidence inspires their confidence.

How do I know this? Well, not only do I talk the talk, I walk the walk. I guess the million-dollar question is how did I give myself a success makeover and become a master of the art of seduction? It's simple: I failed at a lot of things first. And in doing so, I learned that failure is not the end of a road, but just a bend in it. Failure is a crucial part of our learning curve, but the sting of rejection can also point us in a more fruitful direction. As I struggled through the early part of my career, I began to see a pattern as I watched some colleagues succeed and others fail. Not only did the winners individually excel in their hard skills, they all applied the same collection of behaviors, attitudes, and approaches that gave them an edge on the rest of us. They all listened, watched, anticipated, and reacted their way up the corporate ladder. At first, these observations seemed abstract, but slowly, and over time, I recognized the commonalities shared by my peers and I began to formulate my own ideas concerning soft skills and seduction. When the light bulb finally went off over my head, I couldn't believe many of these common sense practices had escaped me for so many years. Once I made changes to my approach at work and implemented the same practices my more successful colleagues used, success was soon mine and this one-time stock broker quickly became a highly in-demand speaker and an expert on strategic communications and soft skills. After years of struggles and many ups and downs, success was finally mine. And the same can, and will, happen to you in just 30 days if you adopt the plan I lay out for you in this book. Have you ever found yourself sitting at your desk, staring out the window of your office contemplating your career trajectory? Or better yet, and perhaps more than likely, have you found yourself staring at the walls of your cubicle wondering just where you should be (and how you've arrived) at this point in your life? If so, this book will prove that you have far greater control over your destiny than you ever imagined and the success you so rightfully crave is only 30 short days away. So, if you are ready and willing to put in 30 days of hard work, you'll be rewarded with a lifetime of happiness and success. This is a trade-off that's just too good to pass up. This is the truth, I promise. I'm not trying to seduce you. Okay, maybe a little. But if you don't read this book, you'll never know.

1

30-DAY MASTER SEDUCTION PLAN OVERVIEW

You must be willing to make major behavioral changes when interacting with other people in order to become a master seducer. Not only that, but these changes must become part of your everyday routine. I know old habits die hard, but committing wholeheartedly to making the changes in this 30-day plan is not only the first step in your makeover, it is the most crucial step in reinventing your business personality. You'll immediately learn the benefits of tempering your natural instincts to speak first—no longer will you always try to get in the first word. You will now approach each encounter with an open mind and a closed mouth—taking your time to assess and observe the situation and reacting to what you are able to take in during this discovery phase. More specific, you will alter your approach in business encounters so that you first and foremost act as a virtual sounding board absorbing the stream of clues, body language, and other valuable insights the person with whom you're engaging is unknowingly sharing. You'll learn to squash your natural instinct to be a one-way broadcaster of information, always trying to sell yourself and gain the upper hand with aggressive and domineering verbal behavior.

Business guru and bestselling author Peter Drucker summed it up best when he said the key is to always "Listen first, speak last." This book will guide you step by step and week by week on how best to adopt this approach and use it to gain an advantage in business dealings as well as in dealings in all other areas in your life. Once you commence with the program I have devised, you'll see that the skills I encourage you to master and the lessons I teach will produce positive results almost instantly. These results may not be grandiose and life-altering, but they will be subtle and beneficial and no doubt result in learning how to seduce more people into doing business with you. Whether you are a one-person sales machine for a Fortune 500 corporation, running a small business, or self-employed—you will find that deploying these business seduction techniques will have you running with a sprinter's speed for success. The beauty of this endeavor is that you'll see results in just one short month.

Why a month? What is so special about four and a half weeks? What makes my promises more genuine than those of a late-night infomercial pitchman? Why do I feel comfortable guaranteeing success? These are all legitimate questions.

Studies have shown that habits and behavior begin to change after one adheres to a new approach for more than 28 days. These new patterns of behavior become ingrained in your mindset over those 28 days, and with each day you begin to replace the old habits with new ones so that by the end of a month, you will instinctively think and act differently. The success makeover I'll guide you through will change all your perceptions and habits around the way you listen, watch, anticipate, and react to the challenges and opportunities you face every day.

Habits need to change (especially bad habits)—that's something I'm certain of. For example, I once worked with a gentleman who was so confident that some lesser-minded individuals might even say he was full of himself. The problem was that he couldn't sell; he was never able to close a deal. And as David Mamet's play *Glengarry Glen Ross* taught us all, a good salesman must Always Be Closing (ABC). My colleague failed at sales because he was so overbearing and always trying to sell himself and everything he had accomplished. What he failed to realize was that all the bluster was completely unnecessary. All he had to do was sell the value of his experience and the inherent benefits of his hard work rather than go on and on about his personal achievements and the mind-numbing details behind his work process. He was overly enthusiastic in telling stories about the glory days of his high school athletic career, the numerous business awards he had won, and the endless talk about his favorite hobby, golf. Yet he was blind to this bad habit. Worse still, he was unable to escape this pattern of behavior. The sad truth is that he was never going to change. He was far from a master seducer and would never achieve such success. Fortunately, by purchasing this book you have already taken the first step in correcting any such behavior, should that be the case.

I will refer to L-WAR (Listen, Watch, Anticipate, and React) throughout this book. The moniker may sound a tad aggressive considering the book focuses on techniques that help you seduce—but what you (we all) must remember is that we are at war. Not just with competitors, whether they are individuals or different companies or businesses. We are at war with ourselves in trying to break bad habits and change the way we communicate, plan, sell, and react. L-WAR is an all-out battle against outdated methods that once worked but are no longer as effective as they once were. Today's soldiers fight with more sophisticated rifles than those used in World War II and the Vietnam War, so it makes sense for you to enter the battlefields of today's business world with the most advanced weaponry. Or as the old saying goes: never show up to a gunfight with only a knife in your hands.

Another apt analogy is for you to approach the 30-day makeover as you would a diet. Like you would with any weight loss program, your success in becoming a master of seduction will require commitment, strength, and dedication to staying the course and adhering to the program. And just as you would in losing weight on a diet, if you are willing to put in the effort, you'll see results and experience success and pride on a daily basis.

LET'S GET STARTED. HERE'S HOW THE MONTH WILL PLAY OUT

Having a great plan is just the first step on your way to Business Seduction. It's a journey and your first step is here...

Weeks 1 and 2

The goal of the first two weeks is to master the two most powerful tools in the L-WAR toolbox—listening and watching. You will begin by making dramatic changes to your normal behavior and adopt an entirely new discipline that may likely go against so much of what you have done before. Picture a smart drone flying over enemy territory or a consummate player in a trendy bar—during these two weeks you are going to observe and monitor the situation around you. You are going to digest the constant stream of data that crosses before your eyes and prepare yourself for the moment of engagement when you seduce your target into the deal. You'll learn to map out split-second strategies, regardless of the situation, that will help you win over friend and foe alike.

You will have assignments to complete throughout this 14-day period as you dedicate the time and energy necessary to learning the skills needed to become a world-class listener—someone who in two weeks' time will become a keen and insightful observer of human behavior and all its peculiarities.

The Hunch

I touched on the importance of learning how to play your hunches in the introduction, but I feel compelled to reiterate, as it is such an integral component of L-WAR. Just as a seasoned teacher can tell when a student's eyes are wandering toward a classmate's test paper without ever looking in that direction, you will likewise develop this type of intuitive skill if you work diligently on improving your listening and watching skills. Hunches are based on supreme experience, information, and knowledge—the type of insight that can be learned only through the powers of observation. Soon, acting on these hunches will not feel at all like guesswork. You'll come to understand that they are based on the accumulation of hundreds of tiny data points that on their own add up to little, but together offer a burgeoning of decision-making power. You'll find yourself entertaining these hunches more and more if you correctly apply the principles of L-WAR and complement them with a variety of soft skills (skills you'll learn much more about later in the book). The reason I stress the importance of hunches is because learning to act on these gut feelings will put you in a position to head off problems before they surface and endear you to clients and customers for keeping them ahead of the competition.

Week 3

During the third week of the program you will experience a turning point. This is when you'll come to better understand all the information that crosses your radar screen thanks to your relentless pursuit of becoming a better observer and listener. At this point, you should be able to determine more clearly why things are happening, what drives people, what the hidden and unsaid messages are (and what they mean), and how you need to reposition your entire approach to achieve greater success in business.

It is the art of anticipating that turns you into a business seducer. By showing you can foresee what happens next, you demonstrate that you are in control. Better yet, you show that you are a step ahead, and by doing so instill confidence in your target, hopefully a prospective client who will see fit to give you his business.

Have you ever been in a situation in which you just knew what someone was about to say. . . and sure enough, they said it? Maybe it was on a date, in a meeting, or watching a movie; whatever the case, it doesn't really matter. What matters is that you were one step, may even two or three steps, ahead of real time. That's where you want to be at all times in business relations—a few steps ahead.

But What Should You Be Anticipating?

The answer. . . everything. Like a director, you need to know exactly how one scene will blend into the next so that you arrive at the conclusion of the film without any unanswered questions. And just as a football coach, you need to be prepared for trick plays so your defense is always at least a few steps ahead of the other team's offense. The business relationship is a game of chess and you must retain a level of foresight, control, and insight to stay ahead of the competition.

After observing your target for a while, you should be able to anticipate his hopes, fears, concerns, dreams, objectives, and (when you're really getting it and starting to lock in) what will come out of his or her mouth next. I once worked with an event producer, and from our first meeting I could tell he was nervous about something even though he never came out and said anything. He was enthusiastic the entire time we worked together but he subtly began revealing in little ways that he was worried that his boss wouldn't like the direction we were taking the program. He never conveyed this sentiment verbally, but I could tell from all of his body language that this was the case. Anticipating this obstacle, I voiced concern and suggested we sit down with his boss to make sure the three of us were on the same page. I set up a meeting and was able to assuage the boss of any fears while at the same time making the event producer come off like a hero by commending him for his creativity and professionalism.

We explore in this section the in-their-shoes theory. Like hunches, I put great faith in this important theory. You develop a strong sense of empathy when you imagine yourself in someone else's shoes because you begin to think and feel the way your target thinks and feels. Only by walking in someone else's shoes can you gain a deep enough understanding and appreciation for the approach you need to use to seduce your target.

Week 4

The final week of this habit-changing month also marks the start of the rest of your life. Now that you are able to comprehend and decipher all the information at your fingertips as well as anticipate what it is your target will want and need, it is time to create the trusted connections and bonds that allow you to go in for the kill. Harkening back to earlier in the chapter and my reference to *Glengarry Glen Ross,* it's time to close the deal. Remember the mantra of the top-fight salesman: Always Be Closing (ABC).

Now it's time to put the skills you've been working on to work and react to everything you have observed, seen, and heard. By this point, you have listened, watched, and anticipated, and because of this, you've likely earned the trust of your target, and the two of you now share a bond because you've taken the time to observe and learn. All you have left to do is react to the immediate needs of your target.

Your reaction moment may not mark the signing of a contract, but you will have gently taken control of the future of this relationship. Whether it's a pay raise, a promotion, a new job, a new contract, or a new level of influence within your group—you will have moved to a far stronger and more successful position. You will be seen in a more admirable and influential light because of the changes you made to your behavior. You will present yourself as someone whom others will not only want to do business with, but someone they feel they *must* do business with—for their own good or the good of their company. Not a bad result for 30 days of hard work.

But don't twist your arm patting yourself on the back just yet. There is still much more to learn. Because once you put the reaction phase of the master plan into effect, it's time to grow your influence and achieve even greater success with the wise use of soft skills and strategic communication. So read on and keep working hard.

This test is designed to discover how well networked you are with your boss or key clients. For each (honest) *yes*, give yourself one point.

You can score a minimum of zero and a maximum of five points for each section. There are four sections containing five questions each. The maximum score is 20.

How much do you know about your boss's or client's family?

1. Do I know his wife's **or** husband's name?
2. Do I know how many kids he or she has?
3. Do I know the name of his or her pets?
4. Do I know where his or her kids go to school?
5. Do I know how long he or she has been with his or her partner?

What do you know about your boss's or client's interests?

1. I know where he or she took his or her last vacation.
2. I know what his or her favorite drink is.
3. I know what his or her favorite off-work activity is.
4. I know how often he or she exercises.
5. I know the last movie he or she saw.

How much do you know about your boss's or client's work demeanor?

1. I know exactly what he or she is angry about and I'm never confused about what he or she thinks the issue is.

(*continued*)

(*Continued*)

2. I know how to tell when he or she is angry without any words being said. I can tell just by his or her body language.
3. I have the type of relationship with my boss or client that he or she can just look at me and I know what he or she wants.
4. There is never any confusion or misunderstanding about any aspect of our work.
5. My boss or client will often share with me his or her frustrations about work and other team members.

What do you know about your boss's or client's objectives?

1. I know exactly what his or her objectives are for the company in the current year.
2. I know exactly what the biggest obstacle is that he or she faces with the business.
3. I know exactly who is considered to be his or her biggest personnel problem in the office.
4. I know exactly who his or her biggest competitor is.
5. He or she will often ask for my opinion before a key meeting.

Answer Key

The Hermit: If you scored between zero and 5 points—You have a lot of work to do. You need to start from scratch.

The Quiet One: If you scored between 6 and 10 points—You have a chance to make a difference in your life by really digging into The Art of Business Seduction.

The Connector: If you scored between 11 and 15 points—You have a decent sense of what it takes to seduce people, but you could use a good bit of extra work to put you into master status.

The Apprentice: If you scored between 16 and 18 points—You are close to being a master seducer—You can almost taste the power.

The Master Seducer: If you scored 19 **or** 20 points—WOW! You know what it takes to get what you want—Keep it up!

2

THE L-WAR
AND SOFT
SKILLS MINDSET

USING INNOVATIVE TOOLS TO BECOME
A MASTER OF BUSINESS SEDUCTION

I know how you're feeling right now. Your engines are revved and you want to burst from the starting line and race into the L-WAR and begin your 30-day journey to becoming a master seducer—someone regarded by business associates and colleagues alike as the ultimate influencer. You want to start your new life as a person who continually shapes and shifts the dynamics of your company and the direction of your chosen business. I understand your excitement. Still, I need you to hold steady on the brakes for a bit longer as I tell you about a crucial set of tools that are at your disposal. (The truth is they have always been at your disposal.) As you'll soon discover, these tools are manufactured out of common sense—but please don't be put off or alarmed by their simplicity. These tools will enable you to subtly influence, build trust, attract interest, and drive deals when used properly. These *soft skills,* as I refer to them, are the key components of strategic communications and the perfect complement to L-WAR. And as understated as their name (soft skills), don't be fooled—learning to use them effectively is often the difference between success and failure in the business world.

Soft skills encompass numerous areas of positive and strategic communication. These skills, when used properly, offer proof that you not just *listen* to the words that come out of someone's mouth, but that you truly *hear* them; proof that you put the interests of others ahead of your own; proof that you understand the needs and objectives of the person in front of you; and proof that being either strongly, or loosely, connected to you will be a rewarding and worthwhile endeavor.

Soft skills are evidence that you have put thought, planning, and care into a particular form of communication, whether it be a conversation or an e-mail. Soft skills provide you with the rare ability to connect and influence others—even forge friendships well beyond the boundaries of a standard business relationship. These skills also help you pitch ideas and convince others that their life will be richer if they do business with you. Soft skills can also be applied equally well to any social situation that involves interacting with another individual, whether that's going on a first date (and wanting to guarantee a second) or attending a party solo and not wanting to be left standing alone in a corner all night. Regardless of the situation, the point is that using soft skills will enhance your life and bring you greater success and satisfaction.

Never forget that L-WAR is the driving force behind you becoming a master of business seduction, but always remember that soft skills are the tools ready to help you achieve this objective.

Soft skills give you the ability to communicate in such a way that you'll get people to do and think what you want without them realizing what you are up to. They cover all of the fundamental aspects of how we interact with others—whether face to face, on the phone, online, or even when written in a letter. (Do people still do this?) Soft skills apply to all details pertaining to your presentation (from your dress code and grooming to the design of your letterhead), body language (both your own and your ability to interpret others), effective greetings, your use of language, and your ability to read the needs and emotions of others. (A good reminder that soft skills complement everything you learn in L-WAR is to always listen to that little bird chirping in your ear that everything feeds off listening and watching.) Your aim in all business interactions is to introduce your promise and potential and all those aspects that set you apart and present you as better than anyone else. Soft skills will help you succeed in this measure.

Every time you have an opportunity to communicate, to exchange ideas, to share stories, to guide opinion, and to influence direction . . . you have an opportunity to win people over. Conversely, you also stand a chance of messing things up or not putting your best foot forward. In such instances in which you underwhelm your target, if a score were being kept you would be on the losing end, always trying to claw your way out of defeat. Executed well, soft skills allow you to persuade people to come around to your way of thinking while believing they came to this conclusion all on their own. They allow you to subtly control the way others perceive you and give you the ability to become a chameleon adapting to whatever a particular situation calls for. In the end, soft skills help you come out on the winning end of business endeavors just about every time.

In the world of soft skills, everyone operates on a finely balanced set of weighing scales. Soft skills are the tiny differentiators that can tilt the scale in your favor or even against you. Think back to grade school science class and the scales they used to teach us all about weight and balance—if one more gram of weight were added to one side rather than the other, the balance was tipped. This is an apt metaphor for how our use of soft skills and strategic communications affects our business lives. You always want to try to tilt the scales in your favor by the way you present yourself.

Every day when you walk into your office and meet with your team, your client, your boss, or your colleagues, the scales are equally balanced with 50 percent of the weight on each side. But the balance shifts as soon as you open your mouth and begin your presentation. Everything you say and do tilts the scales one way or the other—for good or for bad.

The trick is knowing when and how to use soft skills, as well as how to keep score when using the skills in this book. When you do something good, the scale tilts in your favor. When you screw up, the scale goes against you. Again, how do you keep score?

Imagine this scenario: You walk into a boardroom for a meeting and sit next to the CEO. You've never met the man, but remember reading an article about him in an obscure magazine in which he mentioned a fascination with space travel. After formal introductions take place and before the meeting commences, you mention how you were almost a bit late as you were so wrapped up in a just published book about the first moon landing. Without doing anything else, the balance of the scale tilts immediately in your favor. You are now subtly in control of the relationship because you've created an emotional connection or bond without actually revealing what you already knew about your target.

If the scale were equally balanced when you first walked in the door, after you've made this connection with the CEO you go from 50 percent, which is neutral, to 50.1 percent or 50.2 percent. The balance doesn't tip dramatically but it nevertheless does tip. Even the slightest movement in your favor is advantageous. You are now ahead of the game. You're in control and hold the upper hand.

However, when things don't go so well, and there's a conversation that never gains traction, or you arrive a little bit late for a meeting, or you mistakenly identify someone by the wrong name, the scales then start tilting against you because of all of these missteps. Not much, of course, but you begin digging yourself into a hole. Now you go from 50 percent to, say, 49.9 percent or 49.8 percent. The fall from grace seems inconsequential by numerical standards, so you might be thinking, "Who cares?" The problem is, you are no longer in control. Now you've dipped below the 50 percent neutrality equator and will have to work hard to regain the upper hand. This is not an insurmountable task but it is an unenviable one.

Luckily, though, the beauty of effectively using soft skills is that you don't have to do much to make sure the scales tilt in your favor. In fact, you can start tilting scales in your favor long before you step into a meeting or speak to a client.

You sell yourself from the minute you walk out the front door of your home in the morning until you get home in the evening. You sell your ideas, you sell your appearance, and you sell your potential to clients and other business associates. All day, every day, we sell ourselves to the outside world. The simple fact of the matter is we all constantly judge each other.

The harsh truth is that, whether you like it or not, we are all in sales. Yes, that's right, sales. We are relentlessly selling ourselves and our ideas. Regardless of whether you are a marketing professional, doctor, teacher, banker, writer, musician, IT developer ... I've said it before, and I'll say it again: we are all in sales!

I'm fully aware you more than likely did not train to be in sales—and the word *sales* does not appear anywhere in your job description. It might say consultant, adviser, assistant, director, or chief executive officer, but nowhere does it say sales. Society, for one reason or another, has conditioned us into thinking we are not salespeople.

After all, what image do you draw when you imagine a salesperson? Most people probably think of a slick-talking hustler standing in a used car lot trying to talk you into buying a lemon, or an annoying telemarketer constantly calling your home trying to persuade you to buy a set of commemorative plates. Or perhaps an animated infomercial pitchman barking at you through your television about the merits of a watermelon dicer.

No doubt these images make some of you uneasy; perhaps they even make your skin crawl. But if you harbor any aspirations at all of succeeding wildly in business, you can no longer be close-minded when it comes to this 'title'. You need to accept the fact that whatever your profession, and whatever your job title, you are all in sales.

I was recently retained to serve as an adviser for Gillette for a campaign they were conducting in the United States in which they interviewed human resource professionals. Despite the politically correct and open-minded times that we live in, a huge majority of these HR executives—the very people selecting applicants for job openings—said that they definitely judged candidates on their appearance and on how well they sold themselves (and, of course, as it was a Gillette campaign: on how clean-shaven they were!).

The point is a good one and fits very well into what I speak about so often—that we are all on at all times. Whether it is right or not, we are continually selling ourselves, and others choose whether to buy us and our ideas. For the millions of people who do not directly work in sales, this idea is often hard to swallow. They dismiss it as irrelevant in their case, and it is often lost and forgotten. But this acceptance that we are all in sales can often make the difference between the talented artist who forever remains undiscovered and impoverished and the one who secures gallery spaces and receives attention and commissions—and ultimately makes a living as an artist who gets paid.

People look at you and they listen to what you have to say. All the while, as the conversation unfolds, they run an internal monologue asking: *Do I like this person? Do I trust him? Do I want what he is selling? Do I like this person enough to say yes, I'll buy his idea?*

And make no mistake—when I say *selling,* I mean all aspects of business communication. Whether it's walking into your boss's office and asking for a pay raise or sitting with a client and pitching an idea, any encounter in which you are trying to get someone else to do what you want falls under the sales umbrella.

Here's another example. Imagine you are a doctor and a patient of yours who suffers from asthma comes in for an appointment. The patient has been using one of those standard, and somewhat outdated, inhalers for many years. In a bid to try to change the patient's habits, you, the doctor, say, "I would like you to change your inhaler and try this new one, which has just arrived on the market. It will be better for you and you may like it even more than your old one."

After sampling the inhaler and after a bit of rumination, the patient says, "No thanks, doc, I like the one I have. I am going to stick with it." Guess what, even with your medical degree hanging on your office wall and your years of quality care and expert advice, the patient still thought she knew better than you.

The problem is you didn't do a very good job of selling yourself, your recommendation, or the product. The presentation was flat. One of the golden rules is that you will sell more effectively if you make something sound more appealing than it might actually be. I call this the *menu theory*. Think of a restaurant menu and then you tell me which item sounds more appealing: tarragon roasted duck breast on a creamy bed of leeks and mashed potatoes, or bits of dead bird on some vegetables. This example is oversimplified but I hope it serves my point. When it comes to sales, the clear and effective use of language earns you trust and respect and helps you clinch the sale.

One more time, and all together now: We are all in sales!

Soft skills are also an excellent tool to help you earn trust. One of the key ingredients for any successful and longstanding relationship is trust. Trust is a crucial element that bonds two parties together, whether those pairs are: boss and employee, doctor and patient, man and wife, or mother and child. Once trust is established, and both parties feel secure, then the opportunities for business deals and ventures open up once this strong working relationship is in place.

What establishes trust? And how can you earn it quickly so you do not get left on the wayside in today's fast-paced business world?

Let's look at the characteristics of someone you might trust. Someone you trust always looks out for your well-being and also keeps an eye out in the event that you need help in any way. These individuals will regularly change their plans or ideas to suit you and you always know that they will respond to your needs. This is true in both business and life. I trust my assistant because day-in and day-out she always puts my priorities ahead of her own, and I trust my wife because throughout our entire relationship she has always stood by my side through thick and thin and just about any other cliché you can name.

So now that you can identify certain properties of trust, you can start to build trust with your boss, colleagues, clients, and customers. One of the ways to do this is by always making sure these people see the extra effort you are making on their behalf—whether that's working late at the office or ensuring a delivery arrives on time for a customer. Once they see you are willing to put their needs and concerns ahead of your own, you will forge a bond that will be very difficult to break.

The good news is that when you listen, watch, anticipate, and react you also build great knowledge and a stronger business connection based on doing things your target wants to see. Not only does this build trust, but it also instills confidence and faith. You will prove yourself not only to be the right man or woman for the job, but the only man or woman for the job.

This notion of staying a step ahead of the competition is not just empty rhetoric but a must for anyone in business. Once you become yesterday's news or seen as an aging dinosaur unable to adapt to the changing world, you are done. Stick a fork in yourself, because your Christmas goose is cooked. And while we are on the topic of food, in the same way that a diet is only effective if you adhere to it over a longstanding period of time and not for just a few weeks, deploying L-WAR and your new toolbox of soft skills as often as you can will teach you a valuable life discipline, as useful around the house and in social relationships as it is in business . . . know your enemy . . . and know your friends.

Adhering to this mantra allows you to appear to be a step ahead. This is a key business asset. We feel more comfortable with people who spot opportunities early on and people who anticipate bumps in the road and already have a contingency plan in place to get us through the rocky times. By practicing soft skills and adhering to the principles outlined in L-WAR, you will quickly be seen as just such a person.

You'll be the person out ahead of the competition; inspiring confidence in customers and clients, and because of this, your reputation in your industry will grow by leaps and bounds. And a strong reputation is even a more potent means of selling yourself than even the most lavish business card. (Spoiler alert: This is not to say presentation isn't important.) Anticipating someone's needs, wants, or desires, and being able to fill those needs, wants, or desires before he even asks for them not only builds trust and confidence but also initiates a feeling of reciprocity on that person's behalf.

In life, when somebody does something nice for us, when someone goes above and beyond and exceeds expectations, we all feel this need to pay that person back for their generous deed. We feel compelled to return the favor in one way, shape, or form.

If one of your team members stays extra late at work to get a task done, you'll no doubt feel so good about what she did to help you out that you'll probably feel as if you owe her. If you go to a restaurant and your waiter or waitress looks after you with great care—going that one step further than you expected by giving you a glass of extra wine (on the house), bringing you an extra dessert, knocking something off the bill—you'll most likely feel so grateful to her that you'll give her a bigger tip than you normally would for a check of a similar amount.

WHY?

Because we all have this human need to pay people back when they go above and beyond. This behavior should become a habit in your business life and as part of your soft skills seduction kit. Take advantage of the notion of giving extra as a way of getting a return in business to make your world just a little bit easier. In the end, soft skills are all about the other person. The underlying creed is painting such a favorable portrait of yourself with both your words and your actions that the person you are seducing will walk away thinking, "I like this person. I want to do business with him." All your actions should be driven toward making your target's job or life easier and more enjoyable.

So let's reflect for a minute before wrapping up, and look back at what we've learned so far. It's a fairly simple equation when you break it down. When you meld the carefully balanced scales of good and bad impressions with the realization that we are all in sales and the understanding that we all need to go that extra mile to earn the payback bonus—then and only then are you growing closer to comprehending the true power of those tiny little soft skills moments.

In the individual soft skills chapters, we will look at tools you can use regarding networking, language, psychology, and meeting etiquette. You'll learn dozens of instantly ready-to-use ideas, from nods per minute, Never say No, the Three Rs of networking to planting idea seeds, using Obama's speech tricks, and the importance of ending a meeting earlier than anyone expects.

When all is said and done, this book will show you how to apply soft skills to every possible business and social situation: from innovative networking and personal branding ideas to the etiquette of the boardroom; from revealing your elevator pitch to winning business; from proposing your idea to negotiating the deal; from maximizing your payback to understanding the powerful effects of your voice and tone; from the science of *techniquette* to the art of the perfect handshake. This book is your ultimate guide to the little things that make a huge difference, in business and in life.

There is no luck involved in this sort of success: it involves the right preparation meeting with the right opportunity. Now you'll be able to control both.

3

LISTEN

"To listen fully means to pay close attention to what is being said beneath the words. You listen not only to the 'music,' but to the essence of the person speaking. You listen not only for what someone knows, but for what he or she is. Ears operate at the speed of sound, which is far slower than the speed of light the eyes take in. Generative listening is the art of developing deeper silences in yourself, so you can slow your mind's hearing to your ears' natural speed, and hear beneath the words to their meaning."

—Peter Senge

"Courage is what it takes to stand up and speak; courage is also what it takes to sit down and listen."

—Winston Churchill

"A wise old owl sat on an oak. The more he saw, the less he spoke. The less he spoke, the more he heard. Why are we not more like that wise old owl?"

—Chinese Proverb

Why are we not more like the wise old owl? How come we all struggle when it comes to listening—to hearing (and

---

understanding) what someone is really saying? Perhaps it's because in today's society an emphasis is put on speaking well, but rarely are we encouraged to listen well. Our parents reminded us to speak slowly; or not to speak with our mouths full. Teachers told us to sit still and keep our mouths shut. College and universities offer classes in public speaking; but nowhere in the curriculum is there a course that concentrates on listening. As such, we are at an automatic disadvantage when we enter into new relationships. Our tendency is to speak in an effort to impress. Acting this way, though, does not help us learn anything more about this person with whom we will hopefully be doing business. The better tack would be to do as the wise old owl—speak less, in order to hear more.

The L-WAR program will help you change ingrained behavior. Most important, I'll teach you the value of listening before you decide to speak. If you follow my plan, you will quickly come to understand how much you can learn if you let someone else do most of the talking. You'll be able to determine what exactly it is they are looking to gain from the relationship by taking the time to absorb everything they have to say. Once you hear what it is they are actually saying, you'll be able to tailor your response and gain control of not only the conversation, but of the relationship. You'll be seen as someone who can be trusted because you have the best interest of others at heart.

You'll first have to overcome the common perception that listening is easy. It is most definitely not. Listening is an acquired skill that is honed only after considerable and consistent effort. Learning the keys to listening the right way will require you to take a more deliberate approach when you engage in any business or social communication. But if you are willing and able to change old habits, you'll reap many rewards, because listening effectively is the first step in becoming a master of business seduction. And—as is the goal of this book—helping you master the art of seduction will hopefully lead you to great success in business and life.

In any meeting or encounter, the first step is to take in all the available verbal and nonverbal data and other crucial information that comes your way. Only then, as you become more fully informed, will you be in a position to speak more persuasively. Listening to the words that come out of someone's mouth is the easy part; understanding what they mean is the more difficult task. It's only after you fully understand what someone is saying that you'll be able to best judge how to respond to them and adapt your language and behavior to best meet their needs. Listening, then, is a two-part program that includes understanding what someone is saying and then learning how to most effectively respond to what they are saying. Once you become well versed in both of these components will you be able to move on to the next step in my L-WAR program.

IMPORTANT QUESTIONS

One key to becoming an adept listener is to arm yourself with a list of questions to use as a tool to better understand what your customers, clients, and colleagues are saying. Just as a good reporter always strives to answer who, what, where, when, and why in his stories, you should also search for the answers to these particular questions before forming a response.

- What are they saying? Translation: What do they really mean?
- What is driving their message? What are the reasons for this meeting or encounter?

- What would they say if they weren't being so polite or politically correct?
- What are they not saying? (This is often more important than what they are saying.)

You must constantly remind yourself that listening is a journey. It is not a short trip. You must be patient and take in the sights and sounds around you and only then will you safely arrive at your destination and be ready to speak. Another way of looking at it is to accept that listening allows you to paint a fuller picture of the person you are dealing with. If you imagine a nature setting, the words may be the trees but you need to fill in the clouds, mountains, the pasture, and so forth. You need to see everything to gain a fuller appreciation of what the artist was trying to render. In the world of business, the verbal communication you receive is only part of the equation, but the preceding bulleted questions will help you round out the picture.

WELCOME TO THE UNITED NATIONS

Listening to someone's words is often an exercise in being able to translate what is really being said. You'll have to envision yourself as a UN interpreter translating a myriad of languages during a meeting of world leaders. The business or social situation you find yourself in might not be as highly charged as a meeting of UN delegates, but being able to read between the lines and decipher what's being said is a valuable skill for becoming a more evolved listener.

Let's take a look at some examples:

Your boss says, "The presentation needs a little extra."
Potential translation: *The presentation is a mess and needs to be reworked to get the message across more clearly.*

Your customer says, "I like where you are going but we could also try a different approach."

Potential translation: *Your approach might not work and needs changing*.

Your employee says, "I wonder what the traffic will be like later."

Potential translation: *Please let me leave early so I don't have to sit in traffic on the way home*.

Your wife says, "The dog could really use a bath."

Potential translation: *The dog stinks. Give him a bath now*.

A client says, "The ad looks good. How about we try it without the music?"

Potential translation: *I hate the music. The ad will never work*.

Likewise, you should be on the lookout for verbal volleys, which are indicators that what someone is saying is not necessarily what they mean.

If you are engaged in conversation, and someone says, "That's interesting," the truth may be that he finds what you are saying far from interesting. What he really means could be "You're crazy and that's the worst idea I've ever heard." Or if someone prefaces a statement with "As I said before," what she's actually saying is, "Weren't you listening?" Maybe she caught you daydreaming or at a time when your mind was wandering and is now calling your bluff. Alternatively, she needs to see that you have heard and understood the nature of her message and she uses the preface "As I said before" to remind you that she is repeating something that matters to her.

Whether it's tact, fear, politeness, or just avoidance, people will often skirt around what they truly want to say and introduce confused comments that don't help anyone. What's interesting to note is that my military clients never do this. They learn pretty early on that, on the battlefield, if you issue a command such as:

"Not sure, but we might think about launching a three-way attack on the enemy quite soon—but then again we might not yet,". . . no one will be safe. In the armed forces, absolute clarity of instruction and order of command give all soldiers clear and unambiguous confidence in what to do and when to do it. In the rest of the world, this sort of clarity is sadly lacking, and we need to translate what we think is being said, rather than take the words at face value.

Obviously, you need to be constantly aware that what is being said to you might not actually be what is truly meant or felt. Most people understand this, but few deal well with overtly conflicting messages—leaving people desperate to shout, "Just say it."

MULTI-PART APPROACH

I believe there are six keys to becoming a skilled listener. Each step is helpful when used alone, but when used together they give you a fully loaded arsenal to engage with in business and social relationships. This multi-part approach will aid you in forming a fuller picture so you can best specifically deal with each customer, client, colleague, relative, friend, or lover.

EAR-TO-MOUTH RATIO

You have two ears and only one mouth—it's an old observation and the point is wonderfully simple. You should do twice as much listening as talking. This directly relates to what I touched on earlier in the chapter—you need to show patience and re-straint when you enter into a conversation or sit in on a meeting. You must resist the urge to jump in and add your two cents. The great value in spending more time listening than speaking is that you'll learn more about your target. You'll take in more than just the words exiting his mouth—you'll come to understand the hidden meaning and the context in which things are being said. By placing a premium on listening, the full picture I talked about earlier will become clearer to you and you'll be able to dictate your words to meet their needs. You'll build trust and earn respect using the ear-to-mouth ratio. And that trust is one of the keys to business seduction.

IN THEIR SHOES

I discuss this concept throughout the book because it is an effective tool in all aspects of L-WAR. It works well in a variety of circumstances and its usefulness cannot be understated. By putting yourself in someone else's shoes you open your eyes to a new world and a new way of thinking. It allows you to imagine what you would say if you stood in their shoes and what you would want to hear if your roles were reversed. It puts you in a positive position to adapt your actions or tailor your reaction to meet the needs of your client or customer. Like all aspects of listening, putting yourself in someone else's shoes takes patience, as you must take certain considerations before speaking. Imagine your client shows up late for lunch, frazzled by a nasty commute and long morning at the office where he was dressed down by his boss. As he pulls up a chair at the table, he goes off with a stream of complaints about everything from your company's services to the traffic on the freeway to the lofty expectations his boss has for him. Rather than jumping in to defend yourself and your company after your client's initial complaint, if you hold off on your reply and put yourself in his shoes you'll be able to give a more appropriate and measured response as opposed to a defensive and knee-jerk reaction. You'll realize that the pressure he's getting from his boss coupled with the time he spent sitting in traffic caused him to vent it all on you. It had nothing to do with your performance; he was merely looking for a scapegoat to make himself feel better. So because you are aware of his plight, and sympathetic as well, you can say to him, "I know how you feel. My boss comes down on me all the time—and sometimes with no good reason! Just tell me what I can do on my end to get him off your back. And next time, let's do lunch closer to your office, seeing as my schedule is a bit more flexible." Your response shows understanding, connection, and a depth of character. It also demonstrates your willingness to make your client's life easier. This type of seduction he won't soon forget and strengthens the bonds the two of you already share.

This approach also deploys a touch of empathy as well. No matter what level we reach in business, we need other people to demonstrate that they get it. Believe it or not, it pays off to simply reaffirm what someone says to you when they 'reveal themselves' by making an emotional statement.

If they say, "This whole costings challenge is giving me nightmares." You should *not* ignore the stated nightmares revelation by replying, "Well—I'm really enjoying my job right now and with luck I might get that promotion." This approach instantly distances you from that emotional revelation and you fail to latch on to the message and create a better bond.

Your reply should make them feel safe with their announcement and automatically allow them to conclude that you are a trusted partner. A good reply, therefore, might be, "Ugh, those things can totally fill your week. I am sure you will get through it fine. Let me know how I can help you."

PLAYING THE PART

I know what you are thinking: "Oh, come on, I've attended a zillion meetings. I know what I'm doing."

In my world of high level coaching, I often meet people who believe they have the whole thing down; who think they are in control of a situation, and yet, tragically, are not. They believe that what they have to say is truly useful to all around that table and equally impressive. In fact, the more senior you become, the less people will feel comfortable sharing advice and guidance with you. The problem in business is that, all too often, nobody puts these people right when they get it wrong. Few people take them to one side after a meeting is over and say, "I hope you don't mind me speaking directly. You weren't bad in there, but I think most people were a little switched off, and you might have been a touch arrogant. Plus, you must try to listen more."

The problem can become increasingly embedded the more senior you become. Many upper-level players surround themselves (often unwittingly) with 'yes' people. These people are actually doing a disservice to their employer by never helping them see the error of their ways, and as a result, never enabling it to be corrected. The truly smart leaders demand to know their mistakes so that they can continually refine their game. Unfortunately, not all of them do. To ease your way into being a great adviser and confidant, you should offer observations and suggestions as a choice.

"If you think it may be of assistance, I have some observations that may help you further refine your style."

Rather than:

"Good Lord, you were bad—a chimp could do better than that."

"Further refine your style" is an excellent and flattering way to critique someone else. What you are actually doing is telling him that he can be even better rather than revealing that he was simply awful. That is a message anyone should respond positively to.

You'll want to play the part of 'trusted' adviser and confidant with both colleagues and clients. Acting in such a way will set you apart as someone who is able to steer others toward success, and because of this, they will trust you and you'll win valuable points and be in control of the relationship.

WHAT DO THEY REALLY MEAN?

I've already referred to how you must act like a UN interpreter when translating what comes out of someone's mouth. But more than just deciphering the words, you also must understand the context in which something is being said. This will allow you to see things in full view—a crucial element of the business seduction. You'll be able to get in their frame of mind. For instance, if someone says the same thing during a heated debate that she does in a more relaxed atmosphere at a party, it will have a different meaning. You need to be able to take emotions into account as well as other clues that come into play. For instance, if you are at a companywide celebration and your boss comes up to you, having had a drink or two—puts his arm around your shoulder and says, "You're a good man, we need to think about a pay raise for you," you will naturally feel pleased. But you might also guess that it may be the alcohol speaking. However *In vino veritas*—"in wine, the truth" also comes into play. This is clearly something he is thinking about—but maybe not something he can yet actually act upon.

Even though you are at a work function, the atmosphere is relaxed and you need only to smile and agree. But if the next day, he's walking the halls continuing to voice his interest in upping your reward, you must react differently. Now you want to engage in a conversation that moves this concept from an idea into an actual change in numbers in your paycheck. Now, the context is professional, not clouded by drink, not sparkling through a party atmosphere. The more you take context into consideration when trying to understand what someone said, the more appropriate response you'll be able to give.

You must also look for other clues when engaged in verbal communication. For example, you need to be on the lookout for any personal or emotional connections that are drawn. If you discuss the merits of a business idea with someone—that's worth only about one or two points on the business-connection scoreboard. But if you begin to move into more personal territory, that's worth 5 or 10 points more because of the emotional connection made and the degree of trust built.

Let's say you have back-to-back meetings with two potential clients. The first meeting goes well. You give your full presentation, and after you wrap up, the client agrees to do business with you on a trial basis. This is good stuff. You closed the deal and built up your client list. The relationship is off and running. If keeping score, you'd earn one point. You earned a small degree of trust thanks to the client's tenuous commitment.

Then you head down the road to your next meeting. As you work your way through your presentation, the client stops you and begins to talk about his daughter's soccer team and how it's important to him to go to her games; and how he relies on those with whom he does business to live up to their end of the bargain so his business runs smoothly. He lets you know he needs you to make his life easier so he can spend time with his family. The job is yours, but even more important, he has quickly established a strong bond with you by talking about his daughter. This connection is deeply personal, and earns you a good 5 to 10 points because it is so charged with emotion. However, those points are yours only if, during future connections with this person, you mention, in relaxed conversation, interest in how his daughter's soccer team is doing, or their latest game score. You now know what drives this person. You listened to his needs and objectives, and now as a great business seducer, you are using that data to construct comments that he will respond positively to. By allowing the client to interrupt without trying to forge on with your presentation, you let him make his important points but at the same time let him reveal invaluable clues that will help you form a long-lasting relationship.

THE DIFFERENCE

You must understand the difference between showing an interest and taking an interest. When you take an interest, your customer, client, or colleague knows you have her best interest at heart. You are not merely going through the motions as showing an interest suggests. Taking an interest involves making a greater commitment on your part. There are certain things you can do to convince others of this. These are little tricks that convey positivity and go a long way in cementing a relationship.

One way of doing this is to repeat back what you hear. People want to feel that their words matter. They want to be assured that their ideas and contributions count for something. If they are clients or bosses, they want to know that their instructions and guidance will be followed. I'm not saying you have to do this word for word, as if reciting a Shakespeare soliloquy, but if you can paraphrase or transmit back what he said, it will go a long way in convincing your target that you will always put his concerns ahead of your own. Likewise, one of the easiest ways that you can demonstrate that you are listening at a meeting is to take handwritten notes as the person in front of you is speaking. Just the visual demonstration that their words matter to you so much that you need to write them down, will score you points!

NPM—NODS PER MINUTE

Another way to read interest is to observe someone's rate of NPM. In other words, how often he or she nods every minute. This simple gesture goes a long way in affirming that they are wholly engaged in the meeting or conversation. I'll go into the idea of nods per minute in greater detail in the next chapter, but the pertinent thing to note as far as listening is concerned is that it's just as important to deliver nods as it is to receive them when you are the one doing the talking. Nodding does not mean that you agree with everything that is being said, but it does mean that you are engaged by what's being said and you want that person to continue speaking. It's a contagious act that goes a long way toward encouraging the speaker and making that person feel good. Again, you build trust and put yourself in control of the relationship. Nodding is also a sign of approval, a green light for you to keep going. When you observe someone nodding—you know that he is giving you permission to continue. It's a good sign and one you must remain open to. What happens if he stops nodding? I'll tell you later in the book!

EMPATHY

The final element of this multi-part listening program is learning how to show empathy. Like the other five parts already discussed, empathy goes a long way in building trust. By showing empathy, you prove you are not egocentric and put value on the concerns others have. For example, if a customer calls you up to complain about a shipment delay, don't look to just cover your own back to stay in her good graces. Hear her out and then tailor your reaction. Let her know you are not proud of what happened and will do everything you can to make sure this is the last delay she'll ever experience. Likewise, tell her that if she needs you to speak with anyone else to offer an apology or explanation that you'll gladly do so. And of course, look to make it up to her with a small gesture or token that lets her know you value her relationship. And should you ever be in a position when the conversation takes a more personal turn, you need to act accordingly. If a customer is distraught because one of his parents is very ill, let him know you understand how he feels and that you would feel the same way if one of your parents were in the same condition. Offer him some ideas on how best to cope and let him know you'll take care of everything on the business end so he can concentrate on taking caring of his parents. By offering a shoulder to lean on in both cases, you strengthen the emotional bond the two of you share.

You are now on your way to becoming a master of seduction. With your newly honed listening skills, you can expertly navigate your way through the initial stages of new business and social relationships. You'll develop a deeper understanding of your customers, clients, and colleagues as well as friends and relatives, allowing you to build stronger and more meaningful relationships. And with a greater appreciation of what it takes to truly listen and hear what is actually being said, now is the time to study body language and master your observational skills.

LISTENING QUIZ

You should take this quiz after the first two weeks. You can achieve a minimum score of 6 and maximum score of 30. Use the ideas in the book to try to improve your score. Remember: Be honest when answering these questions, and if you are feeling brave, ask your partner to also score you. His results may well be closer to the truth!

I know when, and understand why, my partner is angry with me . . .

1. Never
2. Sometimes
3. Often
4. Usually
5. Always

I am told I'm not listening . . .

1. Always
2. Usually
3. Often
4. Sometimes
5. Never

I know the reason when my partner is in a foul mood . . .

1. Never
2. Sometimes
3. Often
4. Usually
5. Always

When I get home I instantly know how my partner's day has gone . . .

1. Never
2. Sometimes
3. Often
4. Usually
5. Always

(*continued*)

(*Continued*)

How much do I know about my partner's family . . .

1. I know very little about the family
2. I have some knowledge about the family
3. I have a decent bit of knowledge about the family
4. I am very well informed about the family
5. I am one of the people the family calls to talk to

I know my partner's best friends and closest co-workers . . .

1. I don't have a clue
2. I have some sense of them
3. I have a pretty good idea
4. I am sure I know who they are
5. I hang out with them and obviously know who they are

Score—Give yourself the amount of points based on the answer.

Selecting answer 5 earns you 5 points and so on.

Horrible Listener: 6 to 10 points
A Lot of Listening to Do: 11 to 15 points
Midlevel Listener: 16 to 20 points
Making Solid Effort to Listen: 21 to 25
A Great Listener: 26 to 30 points

The same rules apply in business. Use what you learn about yourself here to apply yourself there!

SEDUCTION TAKEAWAYS

Listen in Context

What do they really mean? What does their tone indicate? What different meaning might their words have? What are they not saying? You are a streaming interpreter—a listening post who is taking in data and trying your best to fully understand it all. Always consider the big picture before concluding on the meaning of what is being said.

Face it!

You have two ears and one mouth—try to always use them in that ratio. The content going in radically improves the content pouring out!

Put yourself in their shoes

Always walk their walk. The more you can see life through their eyes, the more you will understand what truly drives them. Listening is so much more than hearing the words—it's adding context and color and considering what you would think or say if you were in their shoes.

React to the NPM

Nods per minute give you a clear indication of whether you should go on or make an emergency stop. Observe their nods and use the clues to guide your progress. Deliver your own nods when you get to a key point of your message and spread the positivity. It works. (I am nodding right now!)

(continued)

(*Continued*)

Show that you have listened

Although this is really part of react, it's worth reminding ourselves that listening is a hugely powerful action, but demonstrating that we have *heard* by occasionally repeating back a concept, fear, hope, or concern really does pay dividends. People love it when they know they have been heard!

4

WATCHING

No doubt, on the surface, the concept of watching seems simple enough. After all, we watch people and things every day. Whether it's your child's soccer game, the other cars on the road when you are driving, or reruns of *Seinfeld* before bed, your eyes are well trained. But are they?

This second step in my four-step L-WAR program, though, is much more than just seeing, or staring blankly at what transpires before your eyes. More specifically, this chapter serves as a tutorial on how to expertly observe the bountiful feast of information that you constantly come in contact with. It's about learning to identify and comprehend body language and eye contact so that you can understand the full message that someone is sending your way. As you'll discover, listening and watching go hand in hand even though they are independent skills. Put these two skills to work in tandem and they will help you gain the upper hand in all business and social relationships.

First and foremost, I teach you here how to read and decipher body language and eye contact. If you are hoping to become a master business seducer, this is a skill you must further develop.

Because as you (and others) try to hide your true feelings by couching the words that come out of your mouth, body language reveals exactly how and what you are feeling. At the moment of truth, when your guard is down or when you are under stress or feeling anxious, your genuine feelings will boil to the surface, courtesy of your body language. As you hone your observational skills, you'll come to learn how understanding body language (as well as being able to deliver positive language) will help you build and gain trust in all relationships.

I want you to enter every business and social encounter with your eyes wide open and your mouth shut. Remember: the chapter is titled watching, not speaking. You must exercise patience as you take the time to process all the information available to you. You must change your behavior so that you are constantly watching people and looking for the slightest clues they are unknowingly serving up that you can use to your advantage. The next time you strike up a conversation or enter a business meeting, think of yourself as a TSA (Transportation Security Administration) agent working at an airport who is (hopefully) always on the lookout for unusual behavior from those people passing through a security checkpoint. Or imagine you are a wildlife documentary filmmaker, who after years of studying lions in the plains of Africa knows their behavioral patterns so well that you always have the camera trained on them at the appropriate time so as not to miss any valuable footage. A key element in your pursuit of becoming a master at business seduction is to learn how to study people as well as the effective TSA agent and the documentary filmmaker.

You'll quickly appreciate that the more closely you study others, the greater the amount of data and clues you'll be able to digest. Now the key will be to determine what information is useful; and what information holds no bearing at all. The more time you spend studying the behavior of your colleagues, customers, clients, and others, the more you'll develop a knack for determining what information you can use to help gain control of the relationship. As hard as people might try to hide their true feelings, people will always reveal what they are thinking and how they are feeling through body language. You'll soon be able to tell if someone is bored, excited, exhausted, interested in you, or 'just browsing' simply from watching body language signals. I show you how to cherry-pick the most vital and revealing elements so that you can expertly assess the behavior of the person you are meeting with, and then shape your response and reactions so as to convince the other person you have his or her best interest at heart—that you care more about this person getting what he or she wants rather than your own interests.

What I hope to show you is the discipline of watching. You'll need to hold back your natural instincts to speak and react. We all want to talk, to sell our ideas, to pitch ourselves as the best man or woman for the job and ultimately see others react favorably to our message. But if you have any desire to become skilled at business seduction and persuasion, you'll need to observe what is being said and how others are carrying themselves so you gain the fullest picture. Only then, when you've had a chance to process the valuable information, will you be able to specifically tailor your behavior in the exact manner that best fits the particular relationship you are engaged in.

Here is a list of some common body movements and how best to interpret them. If you are engaged in a meeting or conversation and you see a colleague, client, or customer exhibit any of these behaviors, you need to understand their hidden meaning and then change your behavior so you can regain control of the relationship:

Rubbing jewelry	Shows impatience or anxiety
Rubbing eyes	Shows someone is tired, bored, or frustrated
Slowly crossing arms	Shows someone feels threatened by what you are saying (or might simply be a bit cold)
Slowly crossing arms in a meeting	Shows someone is trying to block you out from her space
Turn palms out or down	Someone is saying please stop talking and listen
Turn palms out and up or open	Someone is saying, "Honestly, this is all I got or the best I can offer"
Sitting back or hands behind head	Shows someone who believes himself to be in charge and is overly confident
Wringing hands	Shows someone is tense
Clenched fists	Shows someone growing aggressive or losing patience
Finger tapping	Shows someone is bored or running out of time
Finger pointing or jabbing	Shows someone is trying to display strength or is growing impatient

The golden rule for this chapter is to watch first and speak second. Study the body language of your colleagues, customers, and clients so that you can most effectively deal with them. Let me use two examples from my own business dealings to help further clarify my points.

My first story shows how to deal with the Alpha Male. You all know the person I'm describing. He's the boss, the person in charge—the person who struts around the office like a peacock in full plumage radiating a heightened sense of superiority and broadcasting in an overly loud voice. In meetings, he'll often lean back in his chair, put his feet on the desk, cross his arms behind his head, and stare at the ceiling. All these actions declare to onlookers that he is in charge (or at least believes that to be the case).

One time I went to pitch myself to be a keynote speaker at a conference and was ushered into a conference room where seven people were gathered around a table. I'd already met with the CEO of the company but there was another gentleman in the room who clearly thought he was the boss. In this room, he was the alpha male and no doubt the one person who would carry the most weight in deciding whether I should be hired as a speaker. How did I know? When I walked into the room and was being introduced, he was the only one looking down and checking his Blackberry. Within a few minutes, he was the only one sitting back on his chair as if it was one of those La-Z-Boy recliners. He was the only one with a face on him that said, "I've heard all this before." I immediately recognized that I needed to play along, so I shifted gears and began catering my presentation around him. Slowly, I could tell I was winning him over. While not forgetting the rest of the table, I began to focus my eye contact on him and engaged him more than the others as the meeting wore on. When he reacted positively to something I said by leaning forward or nodding approvingly, I pressed on. When he began to pull away indicating he was growing bored, I asked him a question to bring him back into the meeting. Then I used his response later in the meeting to show not only that I was listening but also that I considered his input to be of much importance. I began to gain control of the meeting by gaining the respect of the alpha male. I did not try to dominate or in any way remove his power in the room. He went from sitting back (a sign of being bored or uninterested) to sitting forward because he was fully engaged. (Here's a helpful hint: Never sit too far forward because this hints at desperation and, just as in the dating world, you never want to seem desperate). And because he carried sway within the room, the other folks in the meeting began to echo his enthusiasm and became increasingly engaged as the meeting continued.

The moral of this story is that because I deployed my observational skills before even uttering a word, I recognized that I needed to change my strategy at the start of the meeting to satisfy the alpha male. By giving him the recognition he desired, I created an unspoken level of trust and created the impression that I didn't need their business but it was certainly important for them to work with me, as they would benefit from hiring me to speak at their conference. Ultimately, that's what happened. I was hired to speak to their sales team—partly because at first I didn't say a word but rather took the time to observe.

I had an opposite experience when I was hired to speak at a different conference. There was a woman, let's call her a "Challenged Alpha Female," who was in charge of signing off on the content that was to be delivered by all the speakers, of whom I was one. She criticized all of us in one way, shape, or form and demanded that we all change our presentations to a certain degree. The problem was her actions were so over the top that she alienated all of us. The one thing she singularly failed to do was to take a moment and observe how she was losing goodwill, respect, and control. She was desperately trying to cling to some false sense of power and control with her grand gestures and demands. Such was the darkening mood on the team that her boss stepped in and publicly overruled her. She tried aggressively to guard against giving up power, but what eventually happened was that by trying to control everything and everybody, she was forced to surrender control. This Challenged Alpha Female never took the time to watch. Rather, she jumped into the situation with a strict game plan and did not have the wherewithal to recognize that she needed to change her behavior before ultimately losing complete control of the situation and suffering an embarrassing professional setback.

As this little case study shows, you must be able to think on your feet and adapt to what's unfolding before your eyes. And the only way to do this is to polish your observational skills so that you'll instinctively know how to assess a situation so that you can gain control of a relationship. One way to do this is to put yourself in someone else's shoes. We have already touched on this concept in the previous chapter but it's also an important element of the watching stage of the L-WAR program. You must always carefully consider how your colleagues, customers, and clients are feeling at that exact moment. Before you react in any manner, remember to ask yourself how you would feel if you were in this other person's shoes. What would you want to hear? How would you want someone to react? Couple this thought process with spending ample time observing and you'll be able to customize your approach as how to best deal with specific situations. Your ultimate goal is to create the impression that you are there to protect and serve your colleagues, customers, and clients. You want to create a sense of security and instill in these other people a feeling of power, knowing that you will always be there to take one for the team and keep them safe.

I like to think in analogies—and in many ways, the skill of watching is a little like putting together a fine recipe. The one thing you don't want to do is throw together all the ingredients because you think that will taste just fine and then serve it up without testing it yourself. In fact, the way to put together a winning dish is to taste as you go. Add a little garlic. How is it? A pinch more salt? Still good? Now in go the chili peppers. You keep adding ingredients bit by bit until it tastes perfect. This is how we need to work with our watching skills. Every time you do or say something, take a moment to watch the result. Is it good? Then carry on. Do you see a negative response? Then it's time to add new ingredients!

Understanding context is also an integral ingredient in this stage of the L-WAR program. You need to fully comprehend the circumstances that drive someone's behavior. Obviously, the way someone acts at home translates much differently from the way they behave in a business environment. For instance, if you sit back with your arms folded while watching TV on the couch, it probably means you are relaxed, happy, and satisfied. While, as shown previously, if you sit back in such a manner when in a boardroom or business meeting, you'll come across as an alpha male or female. Likewise, if you extend your arms and turn your palms up when entering your home, you're encouraging someone to come to you for a hug, whereas in the workplace this piece of body language says, in effect, "I'm being open and honest. Please trust me."

EXTREMES THAT SKEW THE DATA

People can act differently when they are working under deadlines or under a great deal of stress. This is not normal behavior, so you need to exclude some of what their body language is revealing. And if you are out having cocktails, people will be more relaxed and loosen up so you can't take all of what their body language is saying at face value. So much of it is being influenced by their surroundings as well as what they are drinking. In tight spaces like an elevator, people are more guarded than usual so you need to ignore their body language. The politics of the boardroom can be tricky to navigate so you need to watch for stress-induced power plays and pay attention to those who show business-linked signs of strength. More importantly, people's statements and language, under these extreme conditions, will also hide a variety of truths. You need to be able to make such context-linked determinations on the spot if you are going to be a master seducer. Learning to recognize these subtle differences will be one of the keys that will bring you success because they will help you gain control of business relationships.

I like to use the story of Estelle Morris as an example of understanding context. Estelle Morris is a former member of the British Parliament who abruptly resigned in 2002 when projected literacy target numbers were not met. The abrupt resignation led most people to conclude she was fired. Strangely enough, at the press conference announcing her resignation, she spoke calmly and said she looked forward to spending more time with her family. But her words did not tell the whole story. She sat poised at a table, but the table had no trimming or dressing around it so those who witnessed the press conference were able to see her coiled legs and tightly squeezed hands. From the waist up she looked calm, but the rest of her body language contradicted this. While her words were full of optimism, her body language showed how very stressed and uncomfortable she felt. If one were to hear the press conference on the radio one might think Morris was indeed happy to move on, but her body language told the full story and showed she was distraught about having to leave office.

So take a moment from now on to consider your own silent display. Are you saying one thing but acting out another? Trying to fully control your body language is nearly impossible—but you can easily stop wringing your hands, rolling your eyes, and taking deep loud sighs. Remember—others are watching you as well. So, try to broadcast the message that you want them to see. Leaning forward when under pressure, calmly nodding and taking notes while breathing slowly, will create a far stronger impression than you sitting back, arms crossed, panting, and shutting down.

Another crucial element to becoming skilled at observing others is learning how to decipher the language of the eyes. I can't emphasize enough how much is said with a glance or a roll of the eyes. While someone may not tell the truth with his words, his eyes may lead you to another conclusion. The more time you spend studying others, the more adept you'll become at reading the story behind the eyes. You'll soon find yourself instinctively reacting to what someone's eyes are doing and then tailoring your reaction so you can capitalize on the knowledge you are now able to process. This is clearly not an accurate science, but there are studies that show that from time to time people will give the game away with an eye movement.

The following is a short-handed guide to interpreting eye contact.

If someone looks up at the ceiling before answering a question it can mean they have no clue. You are not dealing with the sharpest character or they are out of their depth. They are literally looking to the heavens for assistance.

If someone looks down while speaking with you, it means he is either shy or lying—or even worse, he is a shy liar. Either way, this person may not be someone you want to always do business with.

If someone is looking to the left or right, she is searching for information, and this is an acceptable eye movement during conversation.

If someone rolls his eyes, it's pretty obvious that he is fed up with what you are saying. This is a make-or-break moment, and to salvage the meeting you need to stop abruptly and take the conversation in a different direction.

If someone is looking at the door, that's where she wants to head. You need to do a better job of engaging her in the meeting.

If someone looks at his watch, time is very important to this person. You need to wrap up your conversation before he regrets ever having agreed to meet with you. By ending the meeting a little early, you are giving him the gift of time and he will like this far more than having the meeting run late.

If two people are with you in a business meeting looking at each other and nodding, it's their way of saying, "See, I told you he would say that." This sign is normally positive because you are possibly fulfilling their expectations.

Eye contact is a crucial element in all human interactions. It is just as important to give eye contact as it is to observe it. All eye contact must be measured, appropriate, and delivered to the right people at the right time (usually when making key points) to truly maximize its effect. When you connect with someone's eyes during a meeting a number of things occur:

1. You establish a temporary bond, something that pays off as your meeting or conversation goes on. Once established, you can repeat the glance, checking for reaction, response, visual opinion, and interest. This can be very useful when trying to jumpstart a new business relationship. After locking eyes several times with someone during a meeting, you can use your newly acquired soft skills (see Chapters 2 and 7) to approach them after the meeting is over and ask their opinion about something and, in effect, lay down an anchor point that you can use later on to reconnect. If you have made absolutely no eye contact with this person, it will be harder to approach them afterward.

2. You include people in what is going on. It is all too easy for people to feel excluded from a meeting that features dull or irrelevant content. To ensure that these people feel included and part of the session, you should endeavor

to make eye contact with them as often as possible. This makes someone feel that he is an integral part of the conversation or meeting.

3. You keep people awake. There is a temptation, if you are not a star player in a meeting, to simply drift off into a state of boardroom sleep. This is characterized by continuously staring out the window or at the cookies on the table, and worst, by actually falling asleep and slumping forward. When people know that your eye contact will keep consistently swinging around the room and shine on them, they will feel compelled to stay alert and remain part of the meeting.

Now that we've established the importance of making eye contact, the question remains, with whom should you make eye contact? Sometimes in meetings with new clients there will be numerous people present, so you might be confused as to whom to train your eyes on. The answer is: everyone.

A client of mine once told me a story about how his company developed a new video game for one of the major game-playing consoles. The day arrived for the big pitch meeting, and my client had arranged for three key players to meet with the potential buying firm—who brought eight people to hear the presentation.

There was the big boss (alpha male), several intellectual property lawyers, some other bigwigs, and a few folks not as high up the corporate ladder. At least, that's how the setup was described to me. As the meeting went on, the three individuals who developed the game directed all their effort and energy at the big boss. They believed he was the holder of the purse strings and the one who would ultimately make the decision.

Little did they know, the boss never acted alone. The folks not as high up the corporate ladder were there to observe for a reason. After the meeting, by all accounts, the boss turned to these extra players and asked what they had thought—whether this new gaming company could become a partner or not. They felt disrespected because they were not once included in the meeting. This rankled them and concerned the big boss. As a result, they did not win the job.

It is crucial that you remember that everyone sitting in a meeting can affect the outcome of your success. Make sure that you make eye contact with everyone throughout the course of the meeting so that no one feels as if anyone is being ignored. You want everyone to be engaged because this fosters goodwill and trust in potential relationships and leads to personal success on your end.

Another way to create goodwill and positive energy is through nodding. I briefly touched on nods per minute in an earlier chapter, but I'll go into a bit more detail here. The average person nods seven times per minute. If indeed the person you are meeting with nods roughly seven times per minute, this body language is a great indicator that he is engaged by what you are saying. These nods don't necessarily mean he agrees with every word you utter but what they do mean is that he finds you engaging and wants you to continue with your presentation. But you must be sharp enough to realize that if the nodding stops, then your colleagues, customers, or clients are growing bored with you and your presentation. Picking up on this indicator, you'll know that you need to change subjects quickly in order to keep the meeting from coming to an untimely end. This quick thinking on your end will help you seduce this person because he'll go from bored to engaged without any verbal prompting on his end.

Likewise, nodding spawns positivity because it is a contagious act. When you are in a pitch meeting trying to win new business by selling yourself as the next best thing, if the alpha male in the room begins nodding, others will respond in kind and very soon you will have won the whole room over. When a big sell moment arrives and you are trying to close a deal with someone important, you too should nod a few extra times. You'll notice that your target will nod as well (catching your positivity). It won't swing the deal but it can really help! You should try it out.

Just as with eye contact, it is important to deliver the same seven nods per minute when someone else is speaking. This subtle show of appreciation convinces others that you like what they have to say and helps establish the early bonds of trust in the relationship. More than likely, because of the contagious nature, they'll return the favor and begin nodding back at you—and soon enough you will both be in agreement on the terms of a business deal.

Learning how to effectively watch and observe will put you in a position to be a master of business seduction. By putting the first two stages of my L-WAR program into effect, you will be able to gain a full picture of the person you are dealing with. By being patient when first entering into any conversation, meeting, or relationship, and honoring the credo to *listen, watch, and then speak,* you'll learn how to convince colleagues, clients, and customers that their interests are your interests and you'll do whatever you can to help them reach their goals. Now that you are able to translate exactly what someone is saying with their words as well as with their body language and eyes, the next step is to learn how to anticipate and react to all this new-found information that you are processing on a daily basis.

Watch Quiz: Practicing the art of watching at home gives you a safe zone. Circle the most appropriate answer and be honest with yourself. At the end, add the corresponding numbers to the answers to learn your watching skills score!

You know specifically why your partner is mad when he or she gives you a certain look

1. Never
2. Sometimes
3. Often
4. Usually
5. Always

You know your partner's morning routine so well that you could write it down moment by moment

1. Not at all
2. Some of it
3. A decent portion of it
4. Most of it
5. All of it

You know your partner's mood the moment you see her

1. Never
2. Sometimes
3. Often
4. Usually
5. Always

You can describe your partner's favorite outfits in great detail

1. Not a chance
2. Some of it

(*continued*)

(*Continued*)

   3. A good deal of it
   4. Most of it
   5. All of it

You do certain chores without being told what to do with clues left behind (for example, garbage left at the kitchen door, a list of items to buy at the store, and so forth)

   1. Never
   2. Sometimes
   3. Often
   4. Usually
   5. Always

You know what your partner's favorite TV shows are

   1. None of them
   2. A few of them
   3. A good deal of them
   4. Most of them
   5. All of them

Scoring

   6–11   Open your eyes and keep reading.
   12–17 Time to focus. You are seeing, but are you watching?
   18–23 Not bad—now multiply your efforts.
   24–29 Better than most. Your targets better watch out.
   30–36 The eyes have it. You are a master seducer.

SEDUCTION TAKEAWAYS

Engage in active watching

Watching television, movies, and football and baseball games are all mostly passive activities. We watch, we enjoy, and then it washes over us and we move on to something else. When watching *actively*, we are constantly analyzing what we see, comparing it to past experiences, considering context, character, and the whole story. Switch on and record that data stream.

Test your conclusions

When the Israeli national airline, El Al, takes you through their check-in procedures, they ask you a series of questions, often repeating the questions using different wording. The check-in staff are highly trained observers. They will spot, in an instant, any inconsistency, nervousness, or unusual behavior. You need to do the same thing—ask questions, conduct conversation, and *watch the response*. What clues are there? Interest? Ambivalence? Enthusiasm? Concern? Phrase things differently and test the results. With this constant observational monitoring, you will soon be able to select the right ideas to engineer business seduction.

Key signals

Leaning back: Bored, Uninterested, Senior, Alpha.
Nodding: Please continue.
Staring: Please change subject.
Leaning forward: I am interested, you have me engaged.
Checking watch: I have time pressure, please alleviate it for me.

(*continued*)

(*Continued*)

Finger pointing: I need you to show me that you get this.
Finger tapping: Bored, impatient, move on.
Eyes down: I might not be telling you the truth.
Eyes up: I might not actually have a clue.

Adapt to the signals

Whatever you observe, respect it by instantly adapting your behavior or message to ensure that you are making your target's life comfortable. Subtly show that you have read displayed feelings and requirements and you are adjusting what you are doing and saying to match those displayed needs.

Lighthouse of eye contact

Always remember that you are being watched too, so ensure that the people observing you get to see that you care about them as well. In meetings of more than three people, make a conscious effort to spread your eye contact, like a powerful beam from a lighthouse. This way everyone feels like a part of the meeting and you ensure that no one starts drifting off.

5

ANTICIPATE AND REACT

In the previous two chapters, my 30-day plan concentrated extensively on teaching you how to become better at listening and watching when engaged in business and social encounters. Hopefully, you have spent time carefully observing those around you, trying to read between the lines and truly understand what it is they are saying both with their mouths and their bodies. You are now, thanks to the L-WAR strategy, a skilled interpreter—able to decode the cryptic language others speak so that you know exactly what they mean every time they open their mouth.

There is no longer any miscommunication. No longer does the hidden meaning behind someone's statements escape you. When your client asks, "Why does it takes so long to ship a product from the warehouse?" you now know that what he's really saying is, "I want the product to ship faster, so figure out a better way to get the product from point A to point B."

What he is not saying is, "Please explain to me all the workings of your current shipping setup so that I get the full picture as to why everything shows up late!"

If you have followed my plan, you should now be operating on a more advanced wavelength when it comes to deciphering what others are saying. Likewise, you are now more aware of the hidden messages conveyed by someone's body language; and from these subtle gestures and actions you are able to build a more robust and accurate picture of what someone is really saying.

You can use this feast of data to take the next step in the L-WAR plan: anticipate. You will use the information, signals, and content that cross your wires to piece together an instruction manual on how this person operates. Like a brilliantly skilled surgeon, you are now able to fully understand the effect of each incision and the workings of each body part.

Most important of all, and the beauty of the third stage of L-WAR, is that you will now operate in such a smooth and covert manner that the person you are speaking (or meeting) with will be unaware of how you are shaping the encounter. He or she will grow seduced by your charms and actions and quickly determine that you are someone to be known better and someone to be in business with. Your target will conclude, seemingly on their own, that they want to do business with you. Without fully understanding why, they will have that gut instinct that you are a good person, you know what you are talking about, and that you are just the right individual to get the job done.

The changes you will make in the anticipate stage are not grand. Rather, these actions are subtle and almost undetectable on their own. Yet, their effectiveness in helping you gain control of a business relationship cannot be understated. Anticipating is about piecing clues together so that you know the ending to the novel before you're halfway through reading the book. Think of yourself as a world class bridge player studying the other players at the table hoping to learn their tells so you can use these vital pieces of information to gain a competitive tell when they are bluffing from when they are holding a strong hand.

In dating, anticipating means knowing what a person will really enjoy and making sure you offer it up to her before she even asks for it. From earlier observations, you noted that she likes a Pinot Grigio and not a Chardonnay—you peruse the menu and simply say, "They have a nice-sounding Pinot Grigio. Would you like that?" She is loving the fact that you know her. Getting the next date with her shouldn't be a problem.

Learning how to anticipate creates a connection and shows that you understand. It demonstrates you are observant and considerate of the customer's or client's needs. Bottom line: anticipating is the key to seducing your target and getting him or her to *want* to do business with you.

PHASE 1 OF ANTICIPATE—PUT YOURSELF IN THE OTHER PERSON'S SHOES

Imagine you are the CEO of a large corporation. You have a large number of employees looking after you. You travel in style. You conduct countless business lunches and meetings. You orchestrate seven-figure deals. Cool, right? But hold on for a second. What is it *really* like??

The pressure you must face on a daily basis is unimaginable. You have to answer to shareholders who demand that you make cuts to improve profits. Your employees, meanwhile, are desperately pleading with you to keep their jobs in place. Meanwhile, your customer base is shrinking because longstanding clients are signing with the competition because they're getting better prices. And every word you say is scrutinized and torn apart by the media and financial analysts who are just waiting for you to fail so they can tell their audiences, "I told you so."

Both scenarios seem logical; but which one is more accurate? Mull this over for a second.

Now, imagine winning the Mega-Millions lottery. You become a millionaire overnight. You can retire and treat yourself to a new house, fancy cars, and the lifestyle you've always imagined for yourself. This is fabulous. No longer will you live paycheck to paycheck or have to worry about balancing your checkbook. You can purchase everything you always wanted guilt-free. There is just one problem. What about the letters from long-lost relatives begging for money and the angry phone calls from friends and family complaining that you're not sharing your wealth as they had hoped? Also, how do you determine from here on out if people are being nice to you because they like you or because they want your money?

Do you think the dream or nightmare scenario plays out if you win the lottery?

In both scenarios, either version could be true. It depends on the person and the circumstances. Your perception may hold true for some, but not others. It's hard to know for certain if you stay on the outside looking in. Any conclusions you come to are merely the result of guesswork. The point I'm trying to make is that to be a great business seducer—to truly understand someone's wants and needs and what makes them tick under pressure—it is imperative that you view life from their perspective. You can no longer make assumptions based on only your own biases, views, or opinions. You know the old saying about what happens when we assume, but let me remind you of another saying that gets to the heart of what I'm discussing: To truly understand what a man is going through you must walk a mile in his shoes. By adopting this philosophy, you'll develop a keener sense as to how others behave and be able to anticipate how they behave.

**BUSINESS SEDUCTION
IMPROVEMENT EXERCISE**

Imagine you are the next person in line waiting to speak to an airline customer service representative after your flight is canceled. Everyone in line ahead of you has vehemently complained about how the airline has disrupted their vacation and travel plans. Some have promised never to fly with the airline again and one even threatened to have his company ban all employees from flying their not-so-friendly skies.

As you approach the counter, try to imagine how the poor, beaten-down airline employee must feel. How would you feel if the roles were reversed? What would you be expecting? Better yet, what would you want to hear? Assessing the situation with this perspective should guide your behavior.

After the string of disgruntled travelers who just aired their complaints, the customer service rep probably expects you to say, "You suck, and this airline sucks." Knowing this is the case and being sympathetic to her plight, you should say, "I know this must be a nightmare for you right now, and yet I can't believe how composed you are. I'm just wondering whether it would help you if I tried to change to another airline?"

I know what you're thinking right now. You are enraged, late, and stressed out—why bother trying to please (and even help) the airline? This isn't the first time they canceled a flight you were on and it won't be the last. So, no doubt you are still trying to figure out why you should go out of your way to help them solve your problem? These are my thoughts: The effort you expend in putting yourself in their shoes will prove to be that tiny differentiator that could tilt the scales in your favor. Of all those

(continued)

(*Continued*)

passengers who crossed paths with the airline employee, she will remember you in a positive light and go out of her way to help you, whether that means getting you on another airline, giving you a dining voucher, or squeezing you on to the next flight out. By creating the impression that you are more concerned about her problems than your own, you create a bond with her and she now feels as if she is in a position to do something nice for you. In her eyes every passenger looked and sounded the same—all negative, all angry, all self-consumed. By putting yourself in her shoes, you were able to create empathy, which led to a differentiator—setting you apart and then creating an emotional bond—all of which would most likely put you ahead of many of those passengers.

Putting yourself in someone else's shoes is a simple concept that few of us spend time thinking about, and even less time incorporating into our behavior. It's a simple act because all you do is imagine yourself to be the very person standing in front of you. The in-their-shoes philosophy trains you to relentlessly think about the needs, feelings, hopes, and fears of your target regardless of what it is you want and irrespective of your end goals. Acting in such a way will gain you favor and put you in control in your business relationships.

In many ways, happily married couples already understand the importance of the in-their-shoes concept. They appreciate that consistently making an effort to understand what it's like to be their partner leads to a lifetime of marital bliss. An understanding husband knows that when his wife returns from a very difficult day at work or watching the kids she will be tired, stressed, and frazzled. His need will be to care for her and his first inclination will be to make sure there are no further demands on her day. In this idyllic relationship, the wife doesn't need to explain that she is stressed, frazzled, and tired. This is understood and the loving husband simply wants to make life easier for her. Is he loving and generous? Yes. But he is also smart because he earns himself payback credits for later use (I know, I know—cynical . . . but true).

You'll never know a business associate or colleague as well as you do your husband or your wife. You don't spend enough time with them for starters; and nor are you as intimate (at least I hope you are not). That's fine because you no doubt understand the business issues and challenges that your clients and customers face, and as a result, you are able to imagine more precisely what it's like to be in their shoes. The more time you spend trying to appreciate the challenges that your business associates face, the greater the bond you'll create with them and the more likely you'll be able to anticipate their wants and desires.

Putting yourself in someone else's shoes provides you with an additional source of data to use in building a trusting and long-lasting business relationship. Combining the in-their-shoes philosophy with your newly honed listening and watching skills, you are in a position to see the world through their eyes and develop a more complete picture of who that person really is.

Even though you will have a wealth of new information at your disposal to help tip the scales of your relationship, you will sometimes need a touch of guesswork, rather than detective work, to join all of these data points together. But remember, making assumptions and decisions without having a complete understanding of the subject can be tricky. This is especially true of business relationships. Too many people love to jump to conclusions in their rush to get something done. However, in the world of business seduction, trying to get somewhere fast is not always the best tack. An opposite approach is often a better play. Biding your time and allowing the data to come forward and then taking the time to process everything that you see and hear before finally delivering a finely tuned message designed with precision will put you miles ahead of the competition and completely in charge of a business relationship.

Likewise, you'll enjoy more success when dating and your marriage will be more rewarding if you incorporate the in-their-shoes philosophy into your relationships. If you are a guy and see a beautiful woman while out in a bar, you might be tempted to tell her she is extremely attractive—that is, if you get the chance to talk with her. It's a conditioned response, as we, as men, want to let everyone know when we see beauty. In fact, we feel the need to tell the object of desire that we indeed desire her. But if you take the time to put yourself in her shoes, you'll probably decide to take a totally different approach. More than likely, this wonderful-looking woman is told how beautiful she is each and every day. It may be difficult to understand, but being on the receiving end of such compliments has become boring and repetitive for her. The one thing she does not want to hear is how beautiful she is. Instead, stand out from the crowd of suitors and tap into another need she has. Let her know how funny she is or that you love the sound of her laugh or perhaps even compliment her on her shoes. Take the road less traveled and the journey will be more exciting.

Interestingly, many men want to hear the opposite. Women, over the years, have told us we are funny or worse yet, cute. What we want to hear (if only these women would step in our shoes for a minute!!) is that we are the most handsome man she has ever met. This is only true because compliments such as these are something we are just not accustomed to hearing. They are the differentiator. Shallow? Yes. Superficial? You bet. Different enough to be memorable? Absolutely. These comments affect us in a deeper and more impactful way because deep down this is what we want to hear . . . whether we are willing to admit this or not!

Putting yourself in someone else's shoes lets you transplant yourself into their world. This simple act helps you use informed judgments to understand how he is feeling and what he wants out of any situation.

BUSINESS SEDUCTION QUESTION

Your boss is under pressure to make staff cuts. Do you:

A. Keep your head down, hoping this is enough to save you from the chopping block?
B. Try to come up with ideas to help the business generate more money?
C. Offer to help him decide the best candidates to be let go?
D. Pursue new clients and new business while taking on additional tasks?

In my opinion, the best answer is D. At this point, it's not about past performance as much as it is about current attitude. Your boss is sitting in his office fretting over keeping the company afloat while knowing he has to fire existing employees, so by using the in-their-shoes thinking, you can best determine what considerations he'll draw from when making his decision.

So ask yourself, if you were the boss right now, what are the possible considerations that you might have for firing someone?

- Are you a team player?
- Are you able to take on more responsibilities when the staff is cut?

- Can you win more business for the company?
- Are you worth the salary you are being paid?

If these are the deciding factors, you need to check these items off his list—and fast. Go see your clients and strengthen your relationship with them. (Check!)

Make your boss aware that you are out there beating the bushes trying to bring in new business. (Check!)

Volunteer to take on more roles within the company as well as any added responsibilities. (Check!)

Be a team player and hold your own team meetings to discuss new ideas, leads, and cost-cutting programs. (Check!)

Talk about the company as if you have a personal stake in it and create the impression that your main concern is making your boss's life easier. (Check!)

The checklist theory works well. It operates very efficiently in the advertising world. From the classiest ads to the cheesiest infomercials, advertisers attempt to offer us a solution to our current problem or challenge. Need sharper knives? This set will cut soft tomatoes, stringy meat, and fresh onions . . . they will even cut through your shoes (check, check, *check!*) (Although I would suggest that if you are cutting up your shoes with knives, you may have other issues!)

Need a sexier perfume? Look how sexy we have made this one appear! You could be this sexy only if you buy it now.

Need a different treatment for your indigestion? Look at the pulsing red graphic we have created and how we extinguish it with a flowing blue graphic!! Wanna feel relieved? Then buy it now.

You—as a consumer of their advertising—sit there, going "Yes, I have that pain . . . (check); yes, it burns a bit like that (check); *yes,* I need a cooling blue something to get rid of it!!! (Check and sold!!)

This sentiment is at the very heart of this book and business seduction—the key always being to put the concerns of others before your own. This scores you valuable points in any relationship and puts you in control as well as in a position to receive valuable payback credits down the line.

Anticipating: Questions

Being well prepared is a key component in learning how to anticipate what others want and need. You always want to be ready to answer tough questions or face down stiff challenges. Performing such due diligence will put you in a position to survive scrutiny from colleagues, customers, and clients alike when your approach comes into question. A good rule of thumb is to always be prepared to answer the questions you hope are never asked. Anyone can sail a boat when the sea is calm but how many can sail when the waters are rough? If you present yourself as someone who can answer the tough questions, you will earn the trust of those with whom you do business.

When I coach the executives, lawyers, or salespeople with whom I work regularly, there is often a moment when I stop the proceedings and ask each of them: "What is the one question you hope doesn't come up?" or "What is the one embarrassing thing that you pray they don't know?"

There is always laughter at this point in my presentation and suddenly a variety of responses come flooding out. "We failed our last project." "Why are we the most expensive supplier?" "How come we have no other clients buying this service?"

What fascinates me is that most organizations (and often employees) will brush these potential questions aside, believing (or, actually, just hoping) that such concerns will never arise. However, not only do these questions come up often, being prepared to deal with any and all flaws and weaknesses is a smart business strategy. No person or company is perfect, but admitting such and letting others know of your shortcomings builds respect and trust because they see you are always working to improve your performance. As I emphasized earlier in the book, we are all in sales whether we are willing to admit this fact or not. Anticipating the tough questions you might face at some point down the road is one of the ultimate pieces of sales training. What if, during a downturn in company sales, your boss suddenly turns to you and asks, "Why do we pay you more than anyone else at your level?" You have to have an answer.

During an episode of the Emmy-award winning television show *The West Wing*, the show dealt with why President Bartlett, who was running for reelection, wanted to be president of the United States in the first place. One of his challengers was asked the question by a member of the press and fumbled the answer so badly that he effectively ran himself out of the race. This individual was seeking election to the highest office in the land and yet he wasn't prepared to answer why he would want such a job. In real life, former President George W. Bush was famously asked in April 2004 what had been his biggest mistake up to that point in his presidency. The president admitted to not being prepared for such a question, and conceded that he couldn't think of any.

He should absolutely have been ready with an answer along the lines of, "It has been difficult to get our international intelligence a hundred percent accurate and some decisions had to be made quickly that really deserved a little more time, but my priority has always been the safety and security of the people of the United States of America."

The lesson to be learned is that a little preparation will keep you from botching the questions that might make or break your career. Obviously, any answers you give to the million-dollar question are a huge part of your defense plan, but so is the way you deliver the answers. A foolproof answer will solve all your problems and save you any embarrassment. So think long and hard about the questions you'd hate to answer, and be ready to answer them.

Self-Debate

A more advanced version of being prepared for those tough or cynical questions is what I like to call self-debate. I encourage bringing difficult questions up before your customers or clients ever have a chance to. You might think I've lost my mind at this point. Why on earth would I encourage you to raise a potentially damaging issue? Why give them that ammo? I may as well load the gun and point it at my own head. The logic behind this thought process is that you retain more control when you raise the issue yourself and then subtly deal with it. You also score very valuable points, as you will appear to almost have read their mind. When you demonstrate a deep understanding of someone's thought process to the extent that you actually say what he or she is thinking, you leap forward and accelerate the bond of trust and give yourself the upper hand in the relationship.

Okay, so how can you effectively use self-debate? Think for a moment about a trial lawyer. He struts confidently about the courtroom explaining how innocent his client is, but then knowing (or at least anticipating) what the prosecution is going to use as evidence, he brings it up himself! "Here you see an innocent man, someone simply in the wrong place at the wrong time. It could happen to any of us and you can imagine how awful that would be if it were you hauled in for something you didn't do (forced empathy).

"But wait," (he goes on) ". . . today you will be told that my client was seen with the money bag in his hand—ready to make a getaway. And they will be right. My client did pick up the money bag. But he did not look to make an escape. Rather, he tried to discover who the money bag belonged to. Foolish? You bet. Nowadays, trying to be a good Samaritan just seems to get you into trouble. My client is *guilty*, all right. Guilty of trying to do the right thing."

There is a strong possibility the prosecution might never have brought up the money bag; but the defense counsel knew there was the chance it would come into play. Deep down, he hoped this would not be brought to the jury's attention. But to counter the effect of this revelation coming from the prosecutor, the defense counsel chose to bring it up himself, in his own time, under his own control. Now the money bag issue doesn't seem like a big issue that could swing the outcome of the case. If or when the prosecution brings it up later in the case, the jury will be underwhelmed because the defense attorney already refuted this point on his own terms.

If you suspect there is a problem or hurdle that could derail your plans and objectives in any business endeavor or relationship, bring these points up in your own time frame with colleagues, customers, and clients. Then once you bring these issues up, deal with them and move on. Your relationship will be stronger because you were honest and to the point. Actions like this build trust, and with that trust you earn points and control of your relationships.

Anticipate through Research . . . Then Talk the Talk

What is your team leader most likely going to do? What will your client most likely need? How can you keep customers from defecting to competitors? To be prepared to deal with these situations (and others of a similar nature), you must do as much research and reconnaissance as possible so that not only do you understand the full picture, you have the tools at your disposal necessary to solve any such problems.

I recently had a meeting with a law firm in London that is a regular client of mine. Even though I've dealt with them on a variety of issues for quite some time now, I still always feel pressure to win them over every time we meet. I always feel the need to be alert and to continue to earn their trust and approval.

Even though I know this client inside and out and count their senior team as friends, I always go on Google and Bing as well as other industry web sites to search and see if the firm has been in the news as of late. This way, I'm able to drop any valuable nuggets of information into our conversation and continue to appear to be connected and informed.

Before our last meeting, it turned out that they had just merged with an Australian firm. They apparently wanted to merge with a Chinese firm to give them a greater presence in the Far East but for a variety of reasons they weren't able to make this happen. So, before heading into the meeting I took time to strategize and take into account what the merger would mean for the senior lawyers with whom I was about to give media training.

I determined they would most likely be doing more traveling because of the merger. Odds are they'd be going to Australia to meet with their new colleagues. Likewise, they would experience a period of transition as the merger played out. And although the merger with the Chinese firm didn't work, my guess was that they were still looking to do business in that market and the Australia office gave them a closer base to work out of.

I knew this valuable information courtesy of a few minutes spent on Google, and was able to tailor my presentation to take all these points into account. Because I was aware of the merger, I focused my talk on the difficulties companies face when they merge. By dropping focused and highly relevant comments into the conversation during my coaching activities, it appeared like I was *very* switched-on about the firm, almost as if I were a company insider.

Instead of saying, "Oh, I read that you just merged with another firm" (which earns a scant few points), I said, "So, for example, when you head out to Australia to meet the new team, you can send this message" and "Well, on the bright side, China is that bit closer now you have teamed up with the Aussies."

Obviously, there was no way I was in a position to possibly know whether one person or another would ever travel out to Australia, but my comments were win-win either way. If certain attorneys weren't going to be part of the team that traveled to Australia, they would be flattered that I would think they would be candidates for consideration. And for those who were indeed about to pack their bags and fly Down Under for business, I appeared to be fully in tune with their career arc and the firm's plans for them.

My comments were sufficiently relaxed and knowledge-assumptive. They instantly created the impression that I was privy to a lot more information than they probably presumed and therefore I was someone who could be trusted with pertinent details. I left no doubt that I was clearly one of the key players on the team.

Use whatever tools and research are available and gather as much data, news, and even gossip as you can. Then use the nuggets of information in your day-to-day communication with customers, clients, and colleagues. You'll appear connected and in the know. This will boost your profile and give you a stronger presence with those you are working with. Seduction is about playing a role, but it is a role you must rehearse for.

PHASE TWO: ANTICIPATE LEADS US DIRECTLY INTO THE REACT ZONE

Once you understand how to process all the information, clues, and signals that you come across when interacting with other individuals, you owe it to yourself to actively begin anticipating the needs and requirements of your target. Even though achieving your own objectives and goals remains your top priority, you must have the discipline to continue with the L-WAR program. One way to do this is to actively ask questions that investigate the status of your business relationships. Probing questions such as these regarding clients, customers, and colleagues are a good starting point:

- What do they need to hear?
- What do they need to see?
- What is expected of them?
- What pressure are they under?
- What would I do if I were one of them?
- What might they need?
- What will they ask next?
- What were their mistakes the last time they were in a similar position?
- What did they love about my service the last time we did business?
- They say no—but do they mean not this time, never, maybe, or not at that price?

Keep these questions running on a constant loop in your head during the anticipate phase. Prodded by these questions and boosted by all of the other information you've learned to decipher, you should have no problem devising suitable, appropriate, and effective responses for each of the questions listed here.

I conduct an exercise with all of my clients in which I have them anticipate objections to their sell, pitch, or message. But more than that, I ask them to go through the process of dreaming up three or four key objections or pushbacks their clients or customers might throw at them. Then I ask them to come up with a strong answer, solution, or counter that will satisfy those customers and clients.

This exercise consists predominantly of common-sense deductions, but so many of us become wrapped up in what we are selling and how cool and desirable our products are that we forget to consider that people might object to them. You must first and foremost determine what the customer, your boss, or your target may single out as being the greatest problem or hurdle.

BUSINESS SEDUCTION IMPROVEMENT EXERCISE

Your Sell:

I feel promoting me will be of benefit to the team and my clients. I feel I not only earned the promotion but that I will rise to a new level of success with the added responsibilities.

Pushback(s):

You are not ready for the responsibility.

Your Counter:

I understand why you say that, but I supposedly wasn't ready for the last promotion and yet I have shined and proven myself to be a very fast adapter.

If you want to come across as extremely sharp and a master of business seduction, you should combine both of these comments in a self-debate style.

Your Self-Debate Sell:

I feel promoting me will be of benefit to the team and my clients. I can rise to the new responsibilities that will be on my plate. Now, I know you might be concerned that I'm not yet ready for this exciting challenge but I remember the team thinking that I wasn't ready for the last promotion, but I shined in the new role. I will do the same with this promotion as I have proven that I can quickly adapt to a greater role within the company.

Pushback Two:

We simply don't have the money in the budget to give you a raise with your promotion.

Your counter:

Let's look at compensation in three months, but let's start now with the title change. It will give you time to see the instant increase in value I will bring and more time to find some wiggle room in the budget.

Pushback Three:

You review is not for another six months.

Your counter:

Maybe we could call this an interim, temporary, or acting position. We could bypass standard review protocol and then we could look into making it official in six months when the time for my review officially comes up.

You know your business better than your superiors do. You know what all the possible pushbacks might be because you've

(continued)

(*Continued*)

been watching and listening and carefully observing all the dynamics that go into your business relationships. And because you know what they are, you are able to effectively counter whatever arguments they might throw at you. You'll impress bosses and clients with your quick and clear thinking and they'll trust that this is a degree of quality you'll bring to all business dealings. Your observation skills continue to sharpen, and with these new tools at the ready you are able to anticipate and react to any scenarios that might pop up. Training yourself to think like this will prevent molehills from ever becoming mountains and bring you success time and again.

Anticipate Being Googled or Binged

Whether you like it or not, people will search for information on the Internet about you. This is something you can guarantee new clients, new customers, new bosses, and new colleagues will definitely do. We all use the informative search engines to gather the necessary information needed to make effective decisions. In anticipating that this will happen, there are a number of things you need to do.

Check Your Privacy Settings

Facebook is a joy. It's the center of the online social world—to be off it, many would argue, is to be out of the loop—when what you really want is to be *in the loop*. But what you post and publish on your Facebook pages may well be searchable for all to find. People who are not your friends or your forgiving family may well locate a drunken tequila photo or a grainy nighttime make-out picture or worse.

Are you in control of this content? Have you been tagged without realizing it? What will people find when they search for you? You need to know the answers to these questions.

Your online brand is extremely important and something you must protect. It is important to know that outsiders now use this content and personal information to help them come to conclusions about who you are, what you represent, and how hiring or working with you might affect their world.

You must carry out a full audit of your online brand. Google yourself with inverted commas, with references to places you have worked or socialized. See what exists online next to your name. In many respects this is your identity. Double-check the privacy settings on your MySpace, Facebook, or LinkedIn profiles. Now go a step further and start to create content that will emerge at the top of the list when people start searching for you on the Internet—deliberately plant content online in order to influence the conclusions people will draw about you.

Becoming Tweetable

Following your online audit, which is mostly reactive, you now need to take control of your online brand and image and become much more proactive.

Let's imagine that you work in IT. What you want to do, using a variety of tools like blogs, Twitter, Forums, and so forth, is become searchable as someone who is highly knowledgeable about the field. You need to write comments, ideas, or anecdotes about everything from the deployment of IT systems and new user interfaces, to how to quickly train a large staff at a low cost to use a new system.

You need to be seen as a thought leader and someone who shares unique or innovative ideas about your chosen area of expertise. Don't be alarmed if you don't have any original thoughts of your own—it happens. Try to find other interesting and valuable content and tweet, link, or rebroadcast it, not as your own, but simply as something you think others will find interesting.

You'll soon notice something strange begin to happen if you take the initiative and start doing some of the things I discuss here. Despite how cynical we all tend to be, we pretty much believe anything we read. This is a unique human condition that goes back to childhood, or to be more precise, to school. In school, we were handed books that were written by experts and filled with facts. We were told to read these books and then be tested on the material we read. We were conditioned to believe these books contained bibles of truths; and rarely did we question the veracity of the contents. This same dynamic holds true in our adult life as well. If you act like an expert, people will believe you are an expert. More than likely, they will accept what comes out of your mouth (or what you post online) as the final word. Again, seduction is about playing a role, and in this example you play the role of industry expert.

You may not be a tenured professor of sciences, but you do know your world inside and out. It's time for you to share your unique insights and ideas with the outside world. Take time to list 10 things about your job, company, product, or industry that you know will stimulate discussion. Once you have your list in order, go into detail and explain why you are focusing on these points and why others can benefit from it. You will enhance your reputation within your area of expertise by assembling this cache of thought leadership content for all to peruse. So my advice to you is to build your profile and be present, be seen, and be searchable. This will allow you to promote your personal brand to a wider audience. And as you will discover in the networking chapter, expanding your contacts and the number of people willing to recommend your services by word of mouth is a key element of business success.

Even if you feel that you do not have enough unique insight, simply surf around for content that you think may fascinate others and send out links or re-tweets to your contacts. This will position you, once again, as someone connected and in the know.

Make Yourself Tweetable

Twitter is still evolving and will either continue to grow exponentially or implode and evaporate in the blink of an eye. But while it is a popular form of communication, you need to board and ride the tweet-train. You must do as other industry leaders are doing and publish your own little 140 character comments and hope that people find you interesting enough to become your followers or send your tweet on to others (it's called *re-tweeting*). Even if your comments are read by only a few, your online presence grows as you become more searchable and ultimately seen as someone with provocative ideas to share. You then become more prominent within your field, and with that prominence there comes a desire by others to do business with you.

Anticipate in Your Cold Calls

You will have to speak very often to important people on the telephone. These people may well have a great influence on your career and life. If you phone them and begin the conversation, "Oh, hello, this is Mark from MarkJeffries.com. Have you got a minute to speak?" They'll most likely respond "no" because you have provided them with an opt-out to get out of speaking with you.

An opening statement like this gives whoever you are speaking to a choice. When you say, "Have you got a minute?" you allow the person on the other end of the line to say, "No." With that, she can hang up and end the call. You can't backpedal and start stammering, "Oh, all it will take is thirty seconds. I can have you off the phone in no time." It's too late. She's already said no. So, what you need to do is turn the tables and take control of the conversation.

Start by saying, "Hi, it's Mark from MarkJeffries.com. I'm just heading out of the office and I know you're really busy, but I'm going to send you an e-mail shortly, so please have a look at it, and let's chat next week."

This tactic is very shrewd. By saying you're leaving the office, in effect you pre-end the phone call. The person on the other end of the line is no longer nervous that he'll be trapped on the line for an indefinite time because you've made him aware that you have only a moment to be on the phone yourself. You also take the offensive by saying, "I know you're very busy." This little wordplay keeps him from saying, "I'm too busy to talk" because you've beaten him to the punch. These two little tricks just bought you 20 seconds of valuable phone time and the opportunity to impress this individual and hopefully start earning his trust. Plus, you also gain points because of the concise message of your call and the fact that you respect how valuable time is to this person.

Anticipating and reacting are essential skills needed to become a master of business seduction and to achieving success in business and life. By becoming adept at anticipating the needs of your customers, clients, and colleagues, you are then able to react in a style that allows you to answer questions and solve problems before they arise. I've provided examples of how to stay one step ahead of your business associates so that you continue to build trust and maintain control of these relationships. By anticipating and reacting to their wants and needs with lightning speed, your customers will think you're trying to make their lives easier by helping them reach their goals.

But you and I both know this is just the perception. Your main objective is gaining your clients' trust (through a little role-playing, if need be) so you can achieve your own goals. The full arsenal of L-WAR is only available to you after you've learned to change the way you listen and watch when engaged in business and social encounters. It is imperative that you are able take all of the readily available information that comes from someone's speech and body language and use these data to paint a fuller picture of the person you're engaged with in business. Then, and only then, can you anticipate what it is they'll want, and react in the most effective way possible to help them obtain these desires. The main point to remember is that you cannot anticipate and react until you have sharpened your powers of observation. My L-WAR program is the key to business seduction because it teaches effective measures for helping you create the impression that you care most about making others happy. Now with a working knowledge of the heart of my 30-day program, allow me to introduce you to a set of tools I call soft skills, which will help drive the engines of L-WAR and allow you to find ways to seduce customers, clients, and colleagues in every situation imaginable.

SEDUCTION TAKEAWAYS

It's them, not me

Now, for the first time, it's less about "What I need to say" and more about "What do they need to hear?" You are finally going to start using the results of your relentless watching and listening to form your business seduction—and you are doing it all to suit "them"!

(*continued*)

(*Continued*)

Be considerate enough to win

Spending time truly considering what life is like for this person in front of you by putting yourself in their shoes as accurately as possible will give you a great depth of insight. The more you know about every aspect of your target's world, the more you can carefully fashion and shape your business seduction.

Be ready

Every six months, professional pilots are put into a technically advanced flight simulator to sharpen their skills. These simulators are apparently as close to actually flying as one can get. Once flying in these simulators, the pilot has to deal with a range of disasters from burst tires to engine fires to loss of power. These are among the worst events that can happen. Yet, after the simulator session is completed, their training is refreshed and they are ready for anything. This is what we need to do in our business lives. Confidence is created when people see that you can handle anything. So put yourself through that simulator and prepare so that you are always ready to deal with the worst possible scenarios. This is the art of anticipation.

Get there first

When selling any idea, customers who are targets will always push back and object. It might be because of cost, lack of confidence, confusion, or simply lack of interest. However, if you have a gut feeling as to what these pushbacks might be, trust your instincts and be smart and courageous enough to deal with these known issues *before* they are even brought up. When you raise a common concern yourself, it surprises your target and you take the wind out of their sails as you instantly show that you are not bothered by it and that you have enough confidence to introduce the topic yourself.

Anticipate their interest

You are going to be checked out! Make sure that you are in charge of what people find. Go one step further and establish yourself as a thought leader in your field. If you are searchable as someone with views, blogs, or tweets on a chosen topic or your profession, you will instantly deliver a more impressive brand.

6

Voice—Tone, Melody, Control, and the Words You Speak

The more comfortable we become doing our jobs, the less likely we are to admit, or even see, our own shortcomings. Self-awareness can and does decline over time. Many of us are unaware or have simply turned a blind eye to faults and weaknesses, adopting a "Why fix what's not broken?" approach to life. As noted earlier, there is nothing wrong with a healthy dose of inner confidence, as self-assuredness is a key characteristic to being successful. Occasionally, though, like a finely tuned piece of machinery, you need to conduct a self-diagnostic test.

To experience lasting success, you should perform an honest self-audit and then take time to evaluate the findings.

As the United States army is fond of saying, you should always strive to be the best you can be. A catchy mantra for sure, but it does somewhat state the obvious. Yet it is that very thing that often lies right before our eyes that goes unnoticed. The very thing many people overlook when evaluating their own performance is their voice. After all, how often do you hear yourself speak? And if customers or clients, or those with whom you work in the home office, find your vocal presentation boring, grating, or less than convincing, the chances of you raising your game in business are slim. The value you have to offer others will be muffled and hidden by your poor verbal skills; and no matter how refined your L-WAR skills are, if you can't get your point across, your potential will be hindered. Others won't have confidence in you.

Your voice is the single most important instrument in conveying your message. Your voice has many components—volume, projection, diction, pace, and tone—and all the elements must work in sync to effectively articulate your point of view. People won't listen to you very long if your delivery is underwhelming regardless of how powerful your message.

VOLUME

Try to recall the last time you were in a restaurant, on a plane, or anywhere else that people gather in a confined space. I'll wager you heard one or two voices talking above the fray.

I was recently dining with a client, and sitting at the table next to us were three businessmen talking shop over dinner. I had no complaints with the seating arrangement except that I could clearly hear one of the men talking over the others. I heard about the value of the property deal they were working on

($20 million), I learned who he did and did not trust, and I learned that the following weekend he was traveling to Miami to close another deal. Meanwhile, and not that I was eavesdropping, but I never heard a single word from the other two members of the dinner party. I only heard the *"shout lout"*.

Setting aside the rules on dining etiquette for just a moment, this entire broadcast could well have been a major breach in client confidentiality. I could have been a journalist or, worse, a competitor. Always remember the old saying when conducting business in public: Walls have ears and so do we. This gentleman clearly had no idea about his bullhorn voice and his colleagues were clearly too embarrassed or did not feel comfortable enough to call attention to the fact that he was bellowing like an over-excited child on Christmas morning as he carried on with his public pronouncements throughout dinner.

I glanced over several times and pointedly made eye contact, attempting to communicate that I could hear every word he was saying. The gentleman was too busy enjoying the sound of his own voice to acknowledge the reactions of those people around him.

So, for his benefit and for the benefit of others like him, here are three tips regarding volume control. If any of these apply to you, you may want to turn down the volume a bit.

1. Your interlocutors seem to be talking very quietly—subtly encouraging you to join them at that level.
2. People keep staring at you—and you're not famous.
3. Someone approaches you and says, "I thought I recognized that voice."

Unlike the early bird who always gets the worm, the loudest person in the room doesn't always reap rewards. Being loud can be a sign of insecurity, a sign that you are afraid to cede control of the conversation or the situation. If you take nothing else away from your soft skills training, never forget that the key is to make your target feel as if he or she is the center of attention and all your energy and concern is focused on purely on them.

PACE AND DICTION

At the other end of the spectrum from the insufferable shout lout is the individual who whispers or mumbles. Here is someone who is under the assumption that just because he can hear himself, that everyone else can also hear him loud and clear—a bit like an ostrich who, having hidden its head in the sand, believes that no part of his enormous body is any longer visible.

How can you tell if you are someone who whispers or mumbles? If people have to constantly lean in close when you speak or consistently ask you to repeat yourself, then more than likely you'll have to project a little more. Soft skills and strategic communication aim to positively affect and influence others so, like Musak playing in an elevator, your voice should put others at ease. Work hard at finding the right volume, pitch, and sound of our voice and the results may ultimately have you screaming for joy.

MELODY

When you watch TV—especially the nightly news and morning talk shows—you will notice that the anchorperson and hosts all have a certain way of speaking. Their voices are mellifluous. Their words flow in a pattern that sounds attractive to our ears, often filled with phrases like "still to come," "don't forget," and "just ahead."

This vocal embellishment is no accident. Television broadcasters are chosen not only for their appearance but also for the way they sound. A good voice is never monotonous, but rather is punctuated with pauses, punches, rises and falls, and is always delivered in a steady rhythm. Close your eyes and try to imagine Brian Williams or Matt Lauer reporting the news and you'll better appreciate what I'm trying to convey. A rhythmic speech pattern is a key asset when trying to impart crucial information, such as world news, weather reports, or election results; just as it is when trying to close a deal or negotiate a salary increase. If your presentation is filled with enthusiasm, it will be met with enthusiasm.

Whether motivating a group of employees, or addressing a conference room filled with 200 delegates, your aim is always to keep the attention of your audience and have them wanting to hear more. A perfect example of the effect of melody—the rise and fall in your voice—can be seen in how we all speak with dogs.

When you want to attract the attention of your dog, you don't use a dull, lifeless voice. It won't listen, nor will it respond. Instead, you need to adopt a high-pitched and more excited voice that accompanies such promising offers as "Wanna go for a walk?" "Wanna treat? Do you? *Do you?* Yes, you do!" The goal is to arouse the animal's sense of anticipation. Normally, your voice will go way up in pitch toward the end of each sentence. The tone you adopt makes the offer sound so tempting that your dog is skipping around, flapping its little ears, and barking with excitement over your proposal.

I'm not saying you should burst into the CEO's office and scream, "Wanna quarterly financial report?? "Do you? Do you???" But if you believe that you may be at risk of sounding dull from time to time, what you can always do in any meeting, conversation, or interaction is animate your voice. Play around and experiment with various ways you can do this so you don't sound like a yapping dog.

Presentation is a key component of soft skills, and once you learn how to manipulate conversations with subtle techniques like the rise and fall of your voice, you will hold your colleagues, customers, and clients in rapt attention as they hang on to your words, wanting to know more. And once they feel this way, you will have them hooked and ready to do business with you.

BREVITY AND THE SOUND BITE

Media trainers advise those who are going to appear as a television or radio guest to keep it short. In fact, the ideal length for a piece of spoken content is about 20 to 25 seconds. This is known as the perfect sound bite.

Why so? Well, apparently, somebody calculated the attention span of the average remote control–wielding viewer. They concluded that the viewer will stay tuned to a channel or station, listening to a particular message, for approximately 25 seconds before needing to turn the dial or click the remote before boredom quickly sets in.

Smart players in a media-savvy world need to truncate their words in order to guard against losing their potential audience in the attention-plagued society. Politicians do it all the time, and seem to have a particular talent for reducing complex ideas, initiatives, and concepts into a succinct 20-second hit. The same theory holds true for e-mail communication.

You have to be brutally honest with yourself when trying to get your message across. You have to determine what it is you must communicate and take a proverbial axe and chop off the excess so just the essential elements survive. Whenever you have a brief window to get your point across or argue your case, you must do it with succinct and concise language so that the person you're speaking with does not have to wade through a morass of language to understand what it is you are saying.

HOW TO CHOP UP YOUR MESSAGE

Here is an example of not getting to the point ...

A small, furry, black and white cat known to locals and, occasionally some people who live farther afield, as Alfie has, would appear and, despite previous warnings and some degree of training, while wandering freely in a park, which was inadvisable from the start, has somehow and inexplicably, taking into consideration the absolute level of chance involved, tumbled into a well.

This epic story takes up way too much time. There are people who can daisy chain a never-ending group of flowery, unnecessary subclauses together to create the world's longest run-on sentence, seemingly without ever getting to an actual point. Don't be this person. The preceding example is extreme, but long, drawn out, and overly ambitious sentences suck the attention (and life) from your audience. Rely on brevity and get to the point! Your reward will be undivided attention.

PERFECT SOUND BITE ...

Onlookers were shocked to discover that a local cat, Alfie, fell into a well today—once again highlighting the dangers of allowing cats too close to wells.

With minimal fuss or elaboration, this sound bite reaches its point before people mentally check out. Effective communication should always quickly get the message across and not fill the maximum time available.

In business or personal relationships, short is sweet. Be succinct and to the point. If you have a story to tell or a new sales pitch, frame your text around the following questions: "Who?" "What?" "When?" "Where?" and "Why?" If these 5-Ws exclude something you still want to tell, break it out only when your initial pitch has aroused such interest and enthusiasm that your audience is clamoring to know more. Then, you can expand your pitch and provide more detailed examples. This again ties in nicely to the elevator pitch in which you begin with an arresting statement of introduction and then build the base of your pyramid with additional remarks that build upon the opening remark.

Your audience has a short attention span. Inspire people with your vision and clarity of thought. Everyone is short on time, so don't take up any more than necessary. Customers and clients will appreciate a quick and detailed response. They'll respect you as a person of action and as someone who works hard to get right to the point. And because of this, they will trust you to get the job done and see you as someone whom they'll want to enter into business with.

THE POWER OF LANGUAGE

Language helps you gain control of a relationship. The effective use of language helps you persuade others to accept your ideas. This is an important step in building trust and establishing long-standing business relationships.

Here are a few strategies for helping you influence others with language.

Rhetorical Questions

Rhetorical questions create interest and command attention.

Do rhetorical questions work? Do they appeal to people? Can they be a way of creating additional interest? Yes, yes, and . . . yes! Of course, one does not live one's everyday life asking rhetorical questions (certainly not out loud, at least): "Would I like a martini? Yes." "Am I happy to pay these prices? No."

But used sparingly during important pitches, meetings, and presentations, rhetorical questions are an excellent way of reinvigorating your audience and maintaining their interest while painting yourself as an engaging speaker. Facts and statistics can become tiresome and dull, but a direct question needs an answer, a story needs an ending, and in one way or another, we all need closure. A rhetorical question helps facilitate this closure. Rhetorical questions are a fantastic tool to show that you are focused on the key issues at hand. They help you come across as an authority to your listening audience—and with this authority comes trust.

Avoid Saying No

Obviously the word *no* holds negative connotations. When you say "No," people automatically feel as if you are correcting them or putting them down. Whether this is your intent or not, you can come across as superior and condescending. You put the other person on the defensive, making them feel uncomfortable. This tips the scale of the relationship and you lose points because this client or customer feels on edge around you. You might feel that aggressive or dominant behavior, such as this, would put you in control of the relationship but the exact opposite is what happens.

Spin it so your remarks come across as positive if you disagree with someone or need to correct her. Imagine you are in a marketing meeting and someone says the key to reaching your target audience of boys between the ages of 12 and 18 is to appeal to their fascination with literary novels. Don't jump out of your seat and scream, "*No*, you couldn't be more wrong, you idiot!" Instead, try something like this, "I appreciate where you are coming from, but we've devoted a good deal of time to market research, and while you are totally right, boys do enjoy reading literary novels, we have found they have a greater interest in sports and video games. For the moment, I would like to focus on what the research tells us and see how we do." This response does disagree and correct the person's assumption, but it does so in a way that is inclusive and encouraging. This approach will win you friends and new business.

The Power of Three

The Power of Three is when you link three ideas as a means of building to your final and most powerful point. President Barack Obama is a master of this technique, and his speechwriters use it to great effect. During the beginning of his campaign when speaking of his ambition of winning the presidential election and gaining the White House, he said, "We will reach for it, we will work for it, and we will fight for it." The crowd rose to their feet in unison and would have carried him to Washington, D.C. if he had asked. Likewise, after being elected, he addressed the citizens of the United States with this thought: "We are not the red states. We are not the blue states. We are the United States." This man knows how to work a crowd.

The Power of Three turns phrases into rally cries and creates instant enthusiasm. You can use this device in all business meetings to win over and influence clients and customers alike. You'll seduce, satisfy, and succeed, and achieve satisfaction, success, and sincere appreciation for being a master of business seduction.

The eyes may be the window to the soul, but your voice and the words that come out of your mouth are keys to winning over clients, earning the trust of employees, sweeping loved ones off their feet, calming screaming children, and, of course, getting your dog to lie down and roll over.

7

NETWORKING SECRETS

Whether it's beers with friends at the local bar, raising glasses of champagne with the CEO at a work reception, or making small talk with the guy next to you on the treadmill at the gym, these are all networking opportunities. Odds are, you feel awkward using business and social situations such as these as an opportunity to try to drum up new business or build up your contact list. But it's essential that you overcome your trepidation and welcome these encounters, and others, as opportunities to achieve greater success. The more people you know, the better your chances that someone will spread the good word about you and the quality of your work. Keep in mind that an innocent conversation with a stranger might lead to you signing the biggest deal of your life (marriage included) or landing a client or customer you might have considered to be out of your league. In many respects, our network is part of our personal brand, and you have a duty to yourself to build that brand.

Facebook, MySpace, LinkedIn, and other social networking web sites are wonderful tools but they don't represent truly effective business networking. They are good ways to build loose connections and contacts—but until you meet someone in the flesh and are given the chance to impress upon them your entire range of soft skills, the chances of engaging in profitable and long-term business relationship are slim.

Being a strong networker can make the difference between remaining a hard-working employee who blends into the woodwork and is often passed over for promotions and becoming a sparkling, well-connected mover and shaker—someone who continually sets the agenda, always appears comfortable and in charge, and is usually liked by people at all levels.

A strong set of networking skills is equally helpful when attending any party or social gathering as it is with all business encounters. Your ability to talk, and even flirt, with brand new contacts will make you appear all the more attractive. Such are the benefits of business seduction.

One of the keys to successful networking is confidence. You may not naturally possess an abundance of confidence, but it is something you can simulate (or fake if you allow me to be so blunt). As I mention in the introduction, seduction is playing a role, so if you have to act the part of a confident man until you become a confident man, more power to you. And of course, mastering all of the soft skills discussed in this book will go a long way in making sure you possess what it takes to make a success of any business encounter, and to make any social engagement a more enjoyable one. The equation is easy to remember.

Good networking skills + well-communicated confidence
= success

ESSENTIAL NETWORKING SKILLS

Most people don't put much thought into their handshake. They look at it as a simple act. Upon greeting someone, most men extend their hand as part greeting. There's no thought behind the act at all, it's a near involuntary reaction. A recent survey supports this line of thinking, as the results show that 80 percent of people polled responded that they have been on the receiving end of damp, limp, wet, weak, or "bone crushing" handshakes. If this doesn't prove that you should put more thought behind your handshake, then I'm not sure what additional convincing you need.

You won't win points for a solid handshake but you will most certainly lose points for a weak one. Soft skills highlight the importance of first impressions, and a good, strong handshake is an important component in making that initial meeting memorable. People won't bother to remark to their friend, in hushed conspiratorial tones, "Hey, guess what, I just shook hands with that guy, over there and ... it was within expectations!!!" But they certainly will lean over to whisper, "Pssst, that guy has the sweatiest handshake ever, like a piece of salmon. Just gross!!"

Imagine you're attending a publishing trade show and you approach a booth for a printer whom you've been trying to land as a client for a few months. Their contract is up soon with their existing supplier so you have high hopes. But you also know two or three competitors are also roaming the trade show floor looking to give the printer their very own sales pitch. You (and your competitors) are all trying to impress the printer with low pricing and supreme customer service. The difference between the proposals is minimal—so what might turn out to be the deciding factor? Hard to believe, but it might all boil down to that first impression and whether you have a firm or a dead fish–like handshake. A well-executed handshake accompanied by the right eye contact and a pleasant smile makes a great first impression—and for most business relationships, the initial handshake is the foundation on which years of business are built.

What always amazes me is how absolutely no one knows one's own shortcomings when it comes to a handshake. In my keynote speeches around the world, I warm up the audience with a quick piece on the ideal handshake. I have had guys come up to me on numerous occasions and say, "Check mine out! Good, right?" And it was absolutely awful. We don't know about our own mistakes because people never tell us. So, we stumble on in blind faith that we have it right.

Here are the golden rules for a good handshake.

Duration

Two seconds. That's it. No more. Of course, cultural differences sometime apply. For example, someone from the Middle East will often hold your hand for up to three minutes. When traveling overseas, you must learn about any specific traditional greetings or social customs. I can't stress strongly enough the importance of the good first impression, and insulting someone from another country will undercut any chance you have of doing business with him. But in most circumstances, particularly here in the United States and across Europe, a two-second handshake will do the trick.

The Long Shakers

What is up with these people who hold on for dear life? You've finished your handshake, you've weakened your grip in preparation for release, and they just keep on shaking, as if they have no interest in ever letting go.

These individuals are committing two handshake crimes. First off, they simply don't know the acceptable duration for a handshake. Second, these folks have no idea that you have finished shaking hands with them. They aren't interested in you; if they were, they would have already released their grip. Instead, they are so caught up in their own agenda—and whatever bizarre reasons they may have for shaking so long—they just keep going until they are done. What does this say about them as someone with whom to do business? They do things their own way. They have their own agenda. They don't respond well to your needs. Not a good impression. This is a serious offense. One of the rules of L-WAR and soft skills is to make the other person (your client or customer) feel as if all your attention is on her. By extending your handshake for too long, you disregard this rule. In the unlikely event that you are a long shaker yourself, remember to stay aware of the people you are meeting—if they want to stop, so should you.

Early Shakers

Many people suffer from ESS (Early Shaker Syndrome). This is when someone rushes in and just squeezes the tips of your fingers. This is a deeply unsatisfying handshake. You leave with the feeling that you both missed your target. The problem is you're never going to say, "Let's do that again!" It's just too embarrassing.

Early shakers give the impression that they don't think you are important enough to shake hands with properly—as if they are in a hurry to move on and meet someone else. Again, this is not the impression you want to make. You must give, or at least perceive to give, your target your undivided attention. If you feel that maybe you suffer from a case of ESS, correct it the next time by calling for a redo and giving a proper handshake.

Strength

A flimsy handshake is unacceptable from a man. The rule is you should match the strength of the person with whom you are shaking hands. Don't use your handshake to overpower or dominate. This might make you feel superior, but a vice grip will never encourage someone to engage in new business with you; it will more than likely turn him off. He'll see you as so overbearing as to be turned off.

If you are a male and shaking the hand of a female, odds are the woman's hand will not be as strong as yours. So, as you apply pressure, match your strength to her strength. If you're a woman, don't feel the need to use more power than you normally would, but then again don't offer up too dainty a grip, as this will be viewed as a sign of weakness.

One man proudly told me that he likes to turn his hand so that it's on top during the handshake to denote strength and power. All good and well if you want to send the message that you intend to dominate any future business—not so good in the world of L-WAR and business seduction.

Clean and Dry

Men get sweaty palms. There's just no denying this. Please resist the urge to wipe your hands on your jacket or pants moments before shaking someone else's hand. This is for two reasons: you don't look very good as you physically wipe your hands on your own clothes, and it is actually not very effective. Instead, rinse your hands off with cold water if you notice sweaty palms. The water both cools your hands down and acts like an astringent, effectively drying off your palms for a good 20 minutes. If you have a drink in your hand, remember to hold the glass in your left hand, keeping your right hand dry, and ready to shake. These hints may seem simple and obvious but they go a long way in showing how considerate you are. This translates into a customer or client believing you will show the same consideration throughout your business relationship.

In a Time of Swine, Bird, or Any Other Creature Flu . . . Don't Be a Bio-Hazard

Do not offer up your hand if you are in the midst of a coughing or sneezing fit and you have been using it to capture all those germs. Politely explain your situation, and undoubtedly in this time of swine flu fear your guest will appreciate your consideration.

The Wrist Grab

While in the middle of a friendly handshake, don't grab the other person's wrist with your free hand, it's tantamount to social kidnapping. The wrist grab symbolizes ownership over the person you are grabbing on to and creates feelings of entrapment and inferiority in the other person. No one wants to feel trapped—and this is especially true in a business relationship. People want to feel like they are in an equal partnership, not one in which they feel like they are under someone else's thumb.

Eye Contact and the Handshake

You must make eye contact with someone when you shake hands. The same rule applies for when you clink wine glasses during a toast—if you look away, it is said to bring bad luck. I will always remember a TV producer I worked with who would always do the same thing every time he shook my hand. I would arrive at the studio and he would come down to the reception area to greet me. He would reach out to shake my hand and at the very instant of contact, he would look down, almost in shame or deference. This instantly demonstrated a lack of confidence, which I soon learned was part and parcel of his character. He rapidly lost control of the production team, the schedule, and the budget. I'm not saying that had he made eye contact when he shook my hand that things would have been vastly different—but my first impression of him was negative, and clearly so was everyone else's. The producer lost points because he looked away at the moment when he should have been looking right at me, to earn my trust. Rather, he lost that trust in a heartbeat. If the producer had a better understanding of soft skills, he just might be running that station now instead of looking for a new job.

I don't want to put undue importance on the handshake, but you need to give it greater consideration than you have in the past. You can no longer view it as a mindless gesture. Delivering a firm, dry, satisfactory handshake with a clear beginning and a definite end while maintaining eye contact, you are effectively announcing, "Look how good it would be to do business together."

More on the Eyes

Eye contact is an important tool used throughout any conversation. It should be consistent and recurring, but not continuous. It should last long enough—several seconds—to prove that you are giving your attention to the other person, and that you are interested in listening to what she is saying.

In general terms, you want to make eye contact when making or hearing:
- Key points
- Story highlights
- Important details

And, most important, always make eye contact when saying hello, goodbye, or shaking hands.

Reading the Eyes

The eyes are probably the single most expressive part of the face. If you can read the expressions made by those around you, this will give you a subtle advantage in your business and social dealings. I don't necessarily think the eyes are one's window to the soul, but most other people believe this to be true. This being said, it's essential that you make eye contact because these individuals will be studying what you tell them with your eyes.

A slightly raised pair of brows indicates either interest or disbelief. A narrowing of the eyes shows empathy or disgust. A slow roll-up of the eyes to heaven is an indicator that your audience has heard it all before and disagrees or thinks you are full of it. A widening of the eye combined with a single tilted nod of the head subtly directed at someone else in a meeting could mean "I told you so."

If you see someone doing this wide-eyed head nod toward a colleague while you are speaking, you can infer that she had previously predicted what you were going to say and may have even mentioned it earlier as a theory herself. She is in agreement with what you are saying. You can use this to your advantage and appear super smart by saying something like, "This is probably something you have looked at yourselves, and here's why we think it will work . . ." Your client will be dazzled by your mind-reading abilities and feel reassured that you are on the same wavelength: "Wow, she really seems to know what I'm thinking and what we talk about—I trust her judgment; we should give her money." An interaction like that is a perfect example of the use of L-WAR skills. By watching your target, you are able to anticipate how he will react to your shift in the presentation or conversation. This little game of wordplay wins you points and, more importantly, wins you the trust of clients, customers, or colleagues.

Eye Movement

This is something of a gray area but experts tend to agree that the four key directions of eye movement when communicating are up, down, left, and right. They can all have significant meaning.

If someone looks up before she answers a question, it indicates that she has absolutely no idea of what she is talking about: it's the equivalent of looking to the heavens for inspiration. If someone looks down before or during an answer, he is either shy or lying. Perhaps, he is even a shy liar. Neither assumption is good, so looking down should be avoided. It does seem to be acceptable, however, to look off to the side for you to gather your thoughts from time to time. It would look totally unnatural if, while you're trying to remember some statistics, you retained a stony, unbroken death stare at your client.

Of course, this is an overly simplified look at a subtle and complicated subject, so I'm not demanding that you apply these interpretations religiously. But I do urge you to be aware of what you are doing with your eyes and to avoid perpetually looking up or down. And, as ever, be cognizant of the people around you and what their eyes may be telling you. Combine your L-WAR and soft skills and all your customers and clients will recognize that you have their best interests in mind and that their success and happiness is your top priority.

YOU LOOK TIRED

Something that has become quite the talking point at my keynotes and conferences has been the need many people seem to have, which is to pass judgment or comment on another's appearance. I remember recently taking my daughter into school and having the mother of another child stop me to observe that I "looked tired."

She literally halted my day to inform me that I did *not* look good. Why would someone choose to do this? This may sound bizarre, but I am prepared to bet that all of us at some stage within the last year have been told we look tired.

No good can come of this declaration. Once you decide to make a negative comment about someone's appearance—directly to his face—the scales start to tip against you. It's a risky approach, and I advise you to refrain from making comments about another person's appearance altogether!

THE GREETING KISS

There comes a time when your level of acquaintance with some-one reaches such a familiarity that a handshake alone might seem too cold and distant. Normally occurring between a man and a woman, this peck on the cheek accompanies a handshake and transmits a clear message to other colleagues and professional as-sociates that we're not involved romantically, we just know each other quite well, and our relationship is strictly professional.

However, the hello kiss is fraught with danger and must be handled with care. A man typically instigates this greeting. If you are in such a position, you must ensure that the woman on the receiving end has no doubt about what you are doing. To execute the greeting kiss, smoothly lean forward slowly to one side and breathe in at the moment of impact. The last thing you want to do is let out a deep breath all over her face.

There are many secrets to making a strong first impression. The one common denominator all these secrets share is that they make use of L-WAR and soft skills. And by using the disciplines I teach in this book you'll constantly score points, build trust, and maintain successful business relationships. Now, I want to take the next step and go beyond the first impression and guide you further in how to build your network and business.

THE BUSINESS CARD EXCHANGE

On occasion, the handshake will be followed with the exchange of business cards. This is another opportunity to make a favorable first impression. A person's business card is a summation of how they have reached this stage of her career. The next time someone hands you her card, don't just shove it into your suit pocket only to be found by the dry cleaner months later. While small in size and only containing a job title and the name of the company she works for, the card says, "I worked really hard for the last so many number of years to get to where I am, so please take me seriously and respect the level I have attained." A simple gesture on your part, whether it's complimenting the design of the card or admiring its embossing, will go a long way to winning you points with the contact. This brief comment will make her feel special and help build the trust mandatory in any new business relationship.

THE FIVE STAGES OF SUCCESSFUL NETWORKING

I want you to picture the early stages of any new relationship—whether business, social, or romantic—as being established through the successful negotiation of these five hurdles: establishing trust, the sell, the promise, the release, and the follow–up.

Establishing Trust

This is when you attempt to create a common bond during the networking stage. You should first try to find out if the individual you're speaking with knows anyone you know or has worked with anyone you know. The more people who connect with you, the stronger will be the trust. This is how the LinkedIn business networking web site works—showing the connections and creating the trust. If not, you can create trust by convincing them of the quality of your current contacts. You can also discuss restaurants, vacation spots, and hobbies with the hope of discovering shared interests. If you share non-work-related interests, this creates an even stronger bond because the connection is more emotional. Bottom line: you'll earn trust more quickly once you find common ground.

The Sell

While continuing to obey the L-WAR rules—always listening, watching, anticipating, and reacting—this is when you employ your soft skills to sell your own best features. You subtly drop pieces of information into the conversation without being too obvious or arrogant; but the message needs to be strong enough to be heard. For example, perhaps you're a web site consultant, so you might make mention how one of your other clients just enjoyed a large jump in quarterly online sales even in a struggling economy. It's also important that the sell is appropriate, relevant, and interesting. Your sell should leave your target impatiently wanting more. In the case of the web site consultant, she'll want to know exactly how you boosted sales.

The Promise

This is when you promise to call, email, text, or have your people get in touch with their people. It's a promise to form a relationship, however deep or shallow.

As part of the promise, it always helps if you can offer up something of value in addition to following up with them at a later date; this might be additional information or another contact you can recommend to help them with another venture. With the promise of a gift like this, you not only engineer a new link, you leave the recipient feeling like he owes you something—this is always a good thing. Building up your payback credits like this is one of your key networking tools.

A great promise is one in which you suggest introducing your new contact to one of your existing contacts. The idea is that you are giving away something of value. Your existing contact will also be grateful, as you are also providing him with a potential business partner. Both of these contacts, old and new, now feel like they owe you a return favor—and having all of these favors in the bank is like saving money for a rainy day.

The Release

This is just another term for how to wrap up the conversation. Having exit strategies suitable for a variety of networking encounters is just as important as knowing how to engineer an introduction. Remember, last impressions need to be just as positive and memorable as first ones. The release can make or break a relationship just as a first impression can.

The Follow-Up

What good is a promise on which you don't deliver? There's nothing worse than when a level of expectation has been created but nothing materializes. It's a bit like the "I'll call you" line after a one-night stand or "The check's in the mail" line when someone is asking you for money. Even if you decide after the initial encounter that this new contact is not going to be of any use to you, you still must follow up. You must strive to grow your network—and who knows, this person might provide a valuable referral six months down the road.

ESTABLISHING TRUST

You get only one chance to make a first impression. It's an old saying, but it's more important today than ever. The problem is that in a world filled with chance meetings and corporate networking, you rarely have the chance to hold someone captive for an extended time for you to make your best impression on her. Rather, you only have a few seconds to capture her imagination, so if you fumble that chance, there just isn't enough time to change that initial perception of you. In today's world, in which time is money, don't go broke making a bad first impression.

Well Read Is Well Fed

People will always be impressed with how intelligent and well informed you are, or at least, appear to be. You can inspire their confidence and trust when you show that you know what is going on in the wider world.

You should be able to speak with some knowledge about economic news, political events, financial markets, industry trends, celebrity gossip, and local developments. These are the conversational hooks that help create connections with other people and seduce them into being captivated by you.

If, during such conversations, however, you admit to knowing nothing about the topic at hand, you miss an opportunity to create a link and connection with your fellow conversationalists. If you are unaware of a major news story, this ignorance may strike someone as odd, and shatter whatever esteem you may have been developing.

Conversely, at a corporate dinner in Budapest, I was remarkably impressed with a charismatic 60-year-old American man with whom I shared a table. He had wonderful insight into business and finance, but he also spoke with passion about travel, politics, fashion, and, most surprisingly, the TV show *Grey's Anatomy*. He recalled specific scenes that he loved and was able to engage with absolutely everyone around that table on many levels. The man demonstrated some of the finest communication skills that I have ever seen. His job? Head of a global tax practice.

Make it your business to learn about things that have nothing to do with your world. On top of "dragonfly skimming" as many news, sports, and entertainment web sites as you can, get answers to questions such as:

- Who are today's most popular fashion designers?
- What music are people listening to?
- Who won *American Idol* and *Survivor*?
- What is the interest rate?
- What is the stock market doing and why?
- Where and what are people eating?
- What is funny on YouTube?
- What's the latest techno-gadget everyone's talking about?
- Who's making money and who's losing it?

And pick up publications that claim to be opinion leaders, from *The Economist* and the *Wall Street Journal* to *GQ, OK, US Weekly, People, Cosmo,* and *Wallpaper.* To appear well informed, you have only to remember a few topical things on a range of subjects. We live in a sound bite culture, so having a few nuggets of conversational wisdom on a variety of topics will be enough to paint you as a well-read and well-informed person about town.

Don't Let On!

Part of business seduction is the relentless building of confidence. People's confidence in you can tick up and down for many reasons—here is one way to keep it ticking up. If there are gaps in your knowledge—and something is bound to crop up in conversations with which you are unfamiliar—the trick is, don't give yourself away. An old theatrical saying is well worth remembering: They only know you've made a mistake if you act like you've made a mistake.

Never play up your mistakes or gaps in your knowledge. Instead, you should plead the Fifth, because the Fifth Amendment of the Constitution's Bill of Rights allows you to decline to incriminate yourself. I'm not saying you should be dishonest or bluff your way through networking opportunities, because someone who does know about the subject in question is bound to call you out. But, you can carefully disguise your ignorance with a few well-chosen phrases. Here are a few responses you can use when you have no idea what someone is talking about and you don't want to let on that you're in over your head.

For example, when asked whether you have heard of something or a certain someone—Have you read the latest *New Yorker* piece by Malcom Gladwell? or What's the latest with Obama's health care plan?—never answer with an outright negative, even if you draw a complete blank. Instead, say something like:

- I know I've heard of him, but remind me again.
- Ooh, tell me why I know that name.
- I know the name, but I can't remember why.
- I keep reading so many different opinions—I can't wait to see the final plan!
- Well, I have my thoughts, but tell me yours.

You'll neatly sweep over the fact that you don't have much to say on this subject, and will turn the meeting to your advantage by continuing to show interest in the opinions of your target and keeping the conversation moving. Make sure you listen carefully at this point; hopefully, something she says will jog your memory or invite an interesting response of your own. You'll score valuable points with your continued interest in whatever it is your customer, client, or colleague is discussing.

Research Your Target

Before meeting up with key players in business—or people who would like to become key players—search for news stories that might be of interest to them, articles about them, or commentary linked to their industry. Then, once you are rubbing shoulders with them, you can use these conversation starters to gain common ground and build trust. Plan for success and success will be yours. Fortune cookie wisdom for sure, but it is wisdom nonetheless.

MAKING AN ENTRANCE

At any social or business gathering people watch two things: their drink and the door. Let's forget about the glasses of warm wine for a moment and instead talk about the all-important door. The big question is: Are you a commanding presence when entering a room?

Remember, the second you push open the door and enter a room, you are on stage. Business seduction is a performance. Stand tall. Don't slouch. Good posture shows confidence, alertness, and vitality. It also instantly pulls in your stomach and lengthens your neck just in case you haven't lost those extra pounds yet. Your appearance and the image you present are soft skills that cannot be neglected.

Once you walk through the door, you must do a quick scan of the room. Who's there? Who's worth your time? Play it cool and gather intelligence as you proceed from one location to another. Put your newfound listening and watching skills into practice.

Once you spot someone you want to talk to, you must first bide your time like a hunting animal and watch what is going on around your target. Let's assume it's a man. Start making judgments. Simply put, observe and report. What you are actually doing is the L and W of L-WAR—Listening and Watching.

Is he alone and approachable? If so, make your move. Or does he look bored with the person he's talking to? Where are his eyes looking? Is he talking to a man or woman? If it's a woman, walk away. Men like talking to women; it massages their egos. So, bide your time, and when it looks like their conversation is wrapping up, prepare to make your approach.

One-Degree Networking

There is no better way to make a new contact than through someone you already know—in other words, through someone removed from you by one degree of separation. Whether it's the boardroom or the bar, using a mutual acquaintance as a conduit adds potency and implicit trustworthiness to your relationship.

Let's say you're at a conference. Your friend or acquaintance is also present and he is chatting with someone who could be of great value to you. You should greet your friend, allow him to introduce you to his target, and then integrate yourself into their encounter. At this point, having used your L-WAR skills to learn what your target wants to hear (perhaps that you run an effective PR firm, you specialize in a certain type of dentistry, or you are a skilled mechanic), make sure whatever you say to your friend is laced with positive suggestions and information designed to pique the interest of the third party. While delivering your message and knowing that you are being observed, you should smile and nod regularly (remember nods per minute). This will create an additional air of positivity and agreement and will encourage your friend to do the same, which, in turn, will convince your target that you are clearly someone to know. As you've learned, the nodding is a sign of goodwill. And the positive vibes that stem forth help build and maintain trust.

Because you are not selling directly to the target, the perceived threat level is low. The target can listen and come to his own conclusion—which is always far more powerful and effective—and he can decide on his own terms, and without any pressure, just how much he wants to know and learn about you. The fact that someone he knows actually knows you is more than half the battle. Whenever possible, do what you can to engineer these valuable connections.

The Self-Engineered Introduction

This is also known as the who-do-you-know method. It is a slight variation on one-degree networking. Engineer your own introductions to people whenever possible. Remember, if you don't ask, you don't get. So, ask people whom you already know who they know. If any one of their contacts could be of assistance to you, or perhaps form the bridge to the target you really want to meet, then all you need to do is ask. Even if she can't (or won't) help, it costs you little in terms of time or money to find this out.

For example, at a business event, large meeting, or conference, go to the organizers and ask, "So, who's here?" They will be happy to point out people to you. "Oh, there's Joe Harris. He runs that boutique software firm that they're all talking about. Oh, and there's Amy King. She's in charge of marketing communications at International Telecom."

All that remains is to choose your moment to saunter over and put your soft skills to work.

Opening Gambit

All systems are a go and you approach your target. You arrive at the introduction zone. You should be positioned slightly more than an arm's length away; any closer is an invasion of personal space. She'll feel threatened if you get too close and immediately pull away. Too many people breach this comfort zone, making the target feel uncomfortable and jeopardizing any chance of building a relationship. Don't lose points by putting your target on edge.

Start the conversation with a polite smile and use the person's name straightaway. This sounds weird, I know, but simply saying, "Hi, aren't you Amy King? I've been meaning to introduce myself and have been looking forward to meeting you ..." is a whole lot better than plowing straight into the conversation with your own name and opening line. Identifying her by name shows that you may have friends in common. And a name check always makes people feel special: it's a simple but effective act of business seduction. The same holds true of any business correspondence and the need to personalize all communication. It's a light touch but carries great weight.

Once your target responds accordingly, it's time to introduce yourself and offer a handshake. Then begin a conversation that sells you and your value and one that hopefully sets the groundwork for a long-lasting relationship.

Talking to Total Strangers

Identifying common ground gets you off to a flying start and establishes an immediate bond of trust. But what do you do if there is not someone around to introduce you to your target(s)? This situation is a bit more daunting. But even if you can't ascertain if you have any shared interests, remember the one thing you share is that you are both in the same place at the same time. In establishing trust, identifying that initial common ground gets you off to a flying start. Whether at a business or social event, you are obviously trusted as much as anyone else in the room by the people who have invited you.

At weddings, the reason a person will sit and listen to a stranger, and even be more susceptible to flirting, is because each guest feels comfortable in knowing that the bride and groom think highly enough of the other guests to have invited them to share in such a momentous occasion. "Oh, if you know him and I know her ... then we, in effect ... sort of already know each other."

There's a vast range of opening gambits to be played in these situations, depending on the occasion and setting. Comment on the food or the music—anything that is a shared experience between the two of you.

- How long does it take to get a drink?
- Trust me, the shrimps are even better.
- Can you believe the view from here?
- Last time I was in this boardroom, we were clinching the New York deal.
- I can't remember ever seeing a 15-piece band before.

By drawing upon this emotional connection, you are going to develop a deeper trust more quickly because the shared experience is even deeper than any discoveries made during a random conversation.

Sidle Up and Eavesdrop

This approach is based on timing and knowledge. While standing to the side and appearing otherwise occupied, you need to eavesdrop on the conversation between a couple of strangers;

then, when an opening presents itself, jump in and add a little nugget to their conversation so that the three of you begin a lively debate as if you were fast friends. Listen. Watch. Anticipate. React. You'll use all four of the L-WAR skills during this type of encounter.

How to Interrupt

Create the illusion that you are busy on your Blackberry or smartphone or admiring the artwork on the walls. In an ideal world, the conversation you overhear should be discursive. For example, if two people are debating the relative merits of Macs over PCs, or whether *24* is better than *Lost,* you can politely interrupt and offer your view. Of course, if you've been really clever, you will already have identified your preferred target out of the group. Then, regardless of your own personal view, in this debate you can side with that target, and win a new friend. All's fair in love and seduction. Remember, play the role you need to play.

There is, however, always the slim chance that this little pair whose conversation you politely interrupted, might turn around and tell you to get lost. If this happens, smile as if unbothered, pretend that you just received a message on your Blackberry and walk away. Don't worry about the rejection. The confidence that allowed you to step into the conversation will remain unbowed. The fact of the matter is you tried, and only by trying can you achieve your objectives. We already established that networking may be uncomfortable and occasionally put you in awkward situations—but if you are willing to leave your comfort zone, great things just might happen.

The Sell

Okay, so you've made initial contact, introduced yourself to your target, and have engaged in some small talk. But whether talking to a prospective client or potential date, the time will come when you need to sell yourself as someone the target really wants to know and stay in touch with. You want to take the encounter to the next level.

Before concentrating on to how to make a good sell, let's clarify what is not considered a good sell. Selling yourself is not an opportunity to boast about yourself, your qualifications, your most-prized possessions, or your hopes and dreams. Rather, the sell is an opportunity to showcase yourself subtly and tailor information to your particular audience. Remember, you want to seduce your target, and win him over, not beat him over the head.

Here is an example of a sell that simply didn't work. I was hosting a major business networking evening for financial directors. The main purpose of the evening was to do a soft sell to potential clients of the host company's products and services without them actually being mentioned. One of the representatives of the host company launched into his sell by talking about the Ferrari he owns. Fair enough, but the story went on and on, and even worse, he repeated his story from the beginning when fresh faces joined the original audience. Not only was the man a bore, but his story was not relevant to the goals of the evening.

Yes, the gentleman made several social blunders, but even more troubling was that he jeopardized an important networking opportunity with his behavior.

Mistake 1: He dominated the group, preventing anyone else from speaking.

Mistake 2: He failed to notice our total lack of interest and our need to move on. He took so long on the (bad) sell that he didn't even get to the promise and release stages.

Mistake 3: He chose a completely inappropriate selling point. He actually put people off and thus lost potential clients. If his audience had been college kids, young and hungry sales guys, or a couple of giggling 18-year-old girls, he might have impressed someone. But among financial directors whose job is to root out and frown on excess while valuing profitable input, it was a disastrous choice.

The moral of this tale is threefold:
1. Know your audience.
2. Choose appropriate selling points.
3. Read your audience's reaction and then respond to it.

This gentleman was completely unaware how to use L-WAR and soft skills, and because of this blew an important chance to make new contacts. It is essential you make others feel as if they are the center of the universe and not that they are merely guests in your universe.

Be a Movie Trailer

A far better way to approach the sell is to think of it as a movie trailer. I don't know about you, but I often end up preferring the trailers to the full-length movie I've gone to see. A trailer teases you with the best bits of the entire film. The movie company teased you with 30 seconds of foreplay to ensure you would eventually part with your hard-earned money upon the film's release.

I want you to focus on the concept of the movie trailer immediately before and during every new encounter. Ask yourself what you have that may be worth putting in your personal movie trailer. Maybe it's the fact that last year you worked with 5 of the top 10 companies in the world. Or, perhaps you designed the most used web site in retail. Have a few unique selling points ready to pull out whenever the opportunity arises. Tease your target so he'll want to know more. By providing small bits of the best information you have to offer, you guarantee your target will want to learn everything he can to fill out the whole picture.

Planting Seeds

You need to convey your unique selling points to your target in an effective and subtle fashion, not pronounce them as cold, factual statements. The more blatant you are, the more likely it will seem that you are showing off. The subtler you are, the more likely that your listener will demand some additional details.

It's the same for dating and flirting. Claim that you are the best kisser in the world and your target will turn and walk. But mentioning that you happen to think that kissing is vastly underrated and that you think it is something very special, you can guarantee that the person you are talking to will already be thinking about kissing you. You want to convince your target that you are good at something while not having to announce the fact. How else could you believe kissing to be very special unless you really were very good at it yourself? You're not asking for a kiss or forcing a smooch on the other person; instead, you have that person intrigued and thinking about just how nice it could be.

You are planting seeds, not digging in 18-foot trees. As part of your seed-planting mission when it comes to business networking, you need to be certain that your target knows that you work successfully with prestigious clients and companies. If you haven't been introduced by a mutual friend or contact, invoke recent successes and subtly drop in the name of a significant client. Like guilt by association, success by association is an equally strong stigma. Clients and customers will find comfort in the successful working relationships you share with others and they'll want to be part of that same circle of success.

THE JEALOUSY REACTION

The jealousy effect begins when we are children and carries itself through our personalities as adults. When we were young, if we saw somebody playing with a toy, regardless of whether we had any prior interest in playing with that toy or not, we now wanted that toy. For example, say two toddlers are sharing a play space but both are ignoring a red truck in the corner. Once the truck catches the eye of one child and he begins to play with it, the other child immediately wants to play with it as well and throws a fit when he can't because he can now see his friend enjoying something he has not yet tried. The same holds true with us as adults. If we see someone else with something that is of interest to us, then we must get our hands on that very thing. This little bit of business gamesmanship can be very effective in piquing the interest of potential network contacts.

Here are two examples of planting seeds that engineered a jealousy reaction and even led to a bit of payback credit down the line. Not bad for a day's work.

I took the VP of a large consumer group out to lunch and I casually mentioned how a prestigious law firm that was keen to win more business following a recent spate of lost opportunities had hired me to work with some of their senior partners. I focused on the fact that this firm had somewhat bizarrely flown me all the way to Tokyo to meet just one partner, and then back to London to meet everyone else. I knew, as I was telling the story, that some of his sales teams had recently been losing business. I had guessed that he was already thinking of ways to improve the numbers. Suddenly, there I was relating how I had not only guided senior lawyers in the art of winning business in a difficult sales environment, but I was obviously important enough to be flown around the globe to meet with just one individual. As I ended my story, he got his Blackberry out and made a note. He said, "I want you to e-mail me with details of what you could do for us. It's something I have been thinking about anyway."

He believed the idea of my coaching his salespeople had been his initiative, when in truth my words triggered his jealousy—just as I had intended. I knew my sell was done when he proposed we work together. All I had to do now was keep the idea fresh in his mind and set the dates to follow up.

Likewise, I had given a number of presentations to a large pharmaceutical company but was never asked to train their salespeople, even though this was something I had long wanted to do. But I knew I could not come straight out and insist that he use me. He needed to make this decision on his own time. So, during one conversation I mentioned how I trained a group at HSBC, and because they were so happy with the group's results they took me out for a night on the town to celebrate. This collaboration and celebration intrigued my contact at the pharmaceutical company so much that he soon brought me into work with some of his sales staff. He was jealous of the success I had with HSBC and he didn't want to miss out on it any longer, so he decided to be proactive and hire me to train his salespeople. In this instance, the jealousy effect got us both exactly what we wanted even if at the start of this little game I was the only one who knew what was best for both of us.

NAME DROPPING

In the aforementioned stories, I dropped the name of the law firm and bank in passing while telling stories that were already highly relevant to my clients. These particular clients needed to know that they would not be the first companies using me in this way, and knowing the name of the law firm and the bank let them both feel as if they were joining forces with a trusted professional. They drew the conclusion that if a firm as well known as X trusted me, they, too, should feel safe doing the same. By subtly dropping the name of the law firm and bank I worked with, I created the impression that I wasn't as nearly as impressed with their reputation as they clearly were.

THE PROMISE

The promise is all about your promises to your target, not the other way around. The purpose of the promise—apart from the promise itself—is to disarm your target by making no demands on him. There is nothing less effective than forcing someone to make a decision upon first meeting him.

Let's say you sell BMW cars for a living. You meet someone at a function who expresses an interest in driving a Series 7. It's a great lead-in, probably more than you would normally get. But don't jump at it—do not be tempted to see this invite as a guaranteed sale if only you push just a bit further. Don't try to set a date for a test drive or arrange a payment plan. You're moving too fast. The target will likely decline all offers.

The correct way to deal with any initial expression of interest is simply to continue the game. Swap contact details and promise to follow up. The cooler you play it, the more persuasive and genuine you will appear. Clients can smell desperation. Seduction is all about building trust and no one trusts a desperate man.

Offer up some "we coulds" such as: "We could think about arranging a test drive for you," or "Next week, we could pick an afternoon for you to come and wander round the showroom some time." Neither of these choices have any teeth; they don't force an immediate decision or commitment. The target is far more likely to agree to think about coming down to the showroom than to sign a finance agreement while still holding his glass of wine.

You are not looking to exit any networking situation with the business already done, and the contract already signed. Rather, you want to open a door and prop it open until you do your follow-up.

THE RELEASE

You have to continually evaluate how you are doing throughout the course of your entire encounter with your target. You need to know whether you have peaked or if your target has had enough of this first meeting. If she had enough, you must consider an early release. There is nothing more dreaded in a social gathering than being trapped by a bore—remember the mistakes made by the guy with the Ferrari. Your aim is to establish trust, make your sale, and suggest your promise, all before the target loses interest. You want to leave her wanting more, not sighing in relief at finally getting away. Plus, if there ever is the opportunity for another meeting, you don't want your target, upon spotting you across the room, thinking "I would rather have a root canal than get stuck talking to that bore again." If you release early, you give the gift of time and respect that your target has other things to do or people she wants to speak with. You show respect, and because of this, you win points and gain trust. But conversely, hold on too long and you lose points as well as control of the relationship. There is a thin line between success and failure, so use the skills in this book to gain the upper hand in all business dealings.

Releasing Too Late

If your target makes any of the following moves, then you've probably gone on too long, and you are too late with your release.

He suddenly folds his arms—he is putting up a barrier between you and him, saying, in effect, "I don't like you and I don't care."

If his feet are pointing toward the door, that's where he wants to go so he can get away from you.

He checks his watch—he's wondering how much time has elapsed and how much is left.

He takes a deep breath and says, "Anyway"—which translates to "I'm really bored and would rather be anywhere than here."

He sees someone else and makes sure they see him—let's face the facts, he wants to go and talk to her and is hoping she rescues him from your clutches.

If you spot any of these signs and react promptly, there's still a chance you can salvage the networking opportunity. But if you don't, this person won't remember how clever you are, he'll only remember the amount of time and effort it took to pry himself from your overbearing encounter. You'll steal the most valuable commodity he owns—his time—and for this you might not be forgiven.

Closing the Circle

A great way to end a conversation is to come full circle and mention something the person said at the start of your talk. This demonstrates that you have been listening and that you have a witty knack of drawing thoughts together. But more important, it shows the prospective contact that you are interested in what she has to say and finds it worthy enough to repeat. This is a key to establishing trust.

Making Your Exit and Dropping an Anchor!

Make your farewell and leave. The mere fact that you are willing to move on implies that you are not a lonely soul with no one else to talk to, but a busy and confident person who is good to know, and keen to know lots of other people. However, before releasing your targets back into the mix and giving them that valuable gift of time, announce that you will be in touch soon following up on part of the discussion. This "anchor dropping" announcement makes it a little more likely that he will come to the phone when you call. Ensure that whatever you are getting back to him about is something that was part of the conversation and clearly interested you both. It may simply be the address of a cool, new restaurant that he had not heard of or maybe the contact details of a talented assistant who could be of great service.

Important note: When making your exit, don't take three steps and then, in full view of those you've just spoken with, start searching the room for your next target. Not only will you look insincere, you'll give the impression that you grew bored with that person's company. Remember, each one of them must leave feeling like each one was the most important person you met that evening.

In the same way as if you were chatting up someone and then you saw an even more attractive person and you broke off hurriedly to approach this second target, don't be tempted to start a new business conquest while in the midst of the current one—you don't want to appear to be a networking slut.

The Dating Exit

Like a great comedian, you want to leave while things are going really well. Leave them wanting more and they'll surely come back for more. Make certain you have each other's contact details and announce that you will be in touch. Smile, say goodbye, and then, like a phantom, you're gone. This confident disappearing act of yours will build up huge anticipation before your first date. Once again, do not go fishing in the same pond looking for an even bigger catch. Leave the bar, go home, and call it a successful night.

Getting It Right

You know you're getting it right if the final exchanges in your networking conversations go something like this:

Important executive: "Yes, well, that certainly sounds interesting." (Oh dear, he checked his watch, or gestured to someone else over your shoulder with a hello type of wave. He might have even taken a deeper than usual breath.)

You (You saw his signals and are smart enough to respond promptly, well done): "It was really good to meet you, here is my card and I have your details. I tell you what, I'll e-mail your assistant with some potential dates for a meeting and maybe I could pop in with some of those ideas."

Important executive: "No problem, my assistant's name is Sarah. Have a good evening." (You're now shaking his hand.)

This CEO will remember a pleasant and productive encounter. He won't be concerned for his freedom should the chance for another meeting arise. And now, he's expecting your e-mail; and as a bonus, you know his assistant's name.

When networking, as long as . . .

- You stand tall at addressing and being addressed
- You have a confident introduction and a firm handshake
- You keep what you have to say focused and brief
- You name-drop a bit and you use the right type of sell
- You offer an enticing promise and release first . . .

You'll have unlimited success.

LEVERAGING YOUR NETWORK

Your network is a large part of your personal brand. You (we all) are a product of the people we know: family, friends, co-workers, colleagues, customers, and clients. Anyone who can expand your business through relationships, connections, or word-of-mouth is part of your network.

Your network is a living and breathing organism, so nurture it and care for it. Grow your network and you will increase your chances of success. One of your top priorities going forward is to widen your network and learn how to better leverage its power.

Nurturing Existing Contacts

You need to stay on the radar of your past and your clients alike. Reminding people you exist is a bit like getting yourself to pop up like a blip on their radar screen. You may be confident in your belief that you are the best at your desired profession, but others need to be reminded of this from time to time. So, you must find ways to reintroduce yourself to your clients and contacts.

Naturally, the more you can personalize any outreach, the more effective it will be. No one reacts strongly to a message that opens with, "Hello all." There is nothing special about being part of a mass correspondence. Send out a mass e-mail like this and you'll get few responses. Whoever is on the receiving end of such an e-mail will immediately know you're just trolling for business by dropping as many lines in the water at once, hoping for as many bites as possible. It's the same theory as throwing a pot of spaghetti against the wall and looking to see which strands stick. The key to building your network by growing your contacts is to personalize any correspondence. You'll reinforce any emotional connection you have with your target by including a personal touch.

Following Up with New Contacts

You just had a great day networking at a conference or have just met a fabulous connection at a party. You used all your soft skills brilliantly and came away with many valuable leads. You've sold yourself to these prospective clients and customers and have promised to get in touch. Now you've got to follow through and deliver on that promise. But what's the best way to do that?

The 3Rs: Radar/Recall/Reward

This approach allows maximizing your powers of seduction and uses your L-WAR and soft skills immensely. You will put your target front and center and act in such a way that convinces the customer or client that their business is your sole focus. It is crucial when you follow up to make note of the experience the two of you shared and what you promised in return. This will allow you to tailor your follow-up around these details.

Radar

As I mentioned earlier, the first and most important element of this three-point plan is to put yourself on the radar screen. You must remind this potential business partner that you exist and also where you met. Be as specific as possible. You can immediately develop your nascent bond by mentioning this shared experience. In today's business world in which e-mail is the most common form of communication, your opening salvo could read something like this:

> Dear Bill,
>
> It was a pleasure spending a few minutes talking with you at the annual Arts Council Conference. I hope you found the evening as enjoyable as I did.

Recall

The key is remembering something your target said. Preferably, something not necessarily business related. This emotional connection stemming from sharing personal information is much more powerful than any discussion on a myriad of business topics. The more finely tuned your listening skills, the more you'll have to work with. The importance of L-WAR can never be forgotten or underestimated. For the sake of this example, let's say you had a discussion about the television show *Lost*. You might continue your e-mail in this manner:

> Dear Bill,
>
> It was a pleasure spending a few minutes talking with you at the annual Arts Council Conference. I hope you found the evening as enjoyable as I did. I remember you saying how much you enjoyed the television show *Lost*. You must be very excited about the final season.

Reward

The reward is the big finish. This is the payoff that will guarantee you get a response. You provide your target with a valuable resource or interesting piece of information that endears you to him and heightens the level of trust between the two of you. Here's how you might wrap up your e-mail:

> Dear Bill,
>
> It was a pleasure spending a few minutes talking with you at the annual Arts Council Conference. I hope you found the evening as enjoyable as I did. I remember you saying how much you enjoyed the television show *Lost*. You must be very excited that the final season begins airing next month. I came across this web site (www.lostsecrets.com) that contains episode guides, character bios, and spoilers that I thought might interest you. Enjoy the final season of the show and hopefully we'll talk soon.
>
> Best,
> Jacob Sawyer

In one short paragraph, you've built the foundation for establishing a long-standing relationship. You took a brief encounter and turned it into an emotional experience by taking what you observed and heard and using those bits of information to gain control of the relationship. By going above and beyond in your e-mail, your target, in this case Bill, will feel compelled to not only respond to your e-mail but perhaps to do something nice in return as we mentioned when discussing payback in an earlier chapter. You've once again tilted the scales in your favor by gaining points with your thoughtful e-mail.

The Telephone Follow-Up

In some instances, it may be more appropriate to follow up by phone rather than e-mail or letter. Of course, getting someone on the line (or to return your call) can always be challenging, especially since your favorable recollection of the initial meeting might not match your target's sentiments. Regardless, the logistics of a phone call are much more difficult to navigate than those of an e-mail. Pinning down someone's availability, actually getting through to them, and then keeping her on the line long enough for you to get your message across is a formidable set of challenges.

In a follow-up phone call, which is much different from a cold call, the initial contact and a desired interest has previously been established. Nevertheless, the target may still have more immediate and pressing concerns when you call, so as with every bit of business communication, keep it short and sweet.

That said, you still need to keep the person on the phone long enough to move your deal forward. You have to do two things to achieve this:

1. "Pre-end" the call.
2. Pre-empt what she would say.

Pre-ending the call is easy. Start by saying something along these lines:

"Hi, it's Mark from the Jeffries Corporation. I am just heading out of the office and I haven't got long."

By delivering this opening statement, the person on the other end of the line knows she won't be trapped on the line for too long.

Pre-empting what she might say is also a straightforward tactic. You continue by saying something like this:

"I know you are very busy, but I just wanted to let you know . . ."

By acknowledging that you already know she is very busy, she cannot use this as an excuse to brush you off. These clever tricks will buy you 20 to 30 seconds of valuable phone time to alert the person at the other end of the line about an incoming e-mail or an important document that will shortly cross her desk. You can also use this call to lay an anchor of return; announcing that you will call again next week or later in the month. A statement such as this leaves the door you're trying to get in wedged open a bit further.

Whether on the phone, face to face, or in an e-mail, a strategic communicator uses powerful soft skills in always considering what the other person wants and needs before delivering his message. So don't forget to dial up your powers of seduction.

Following Up the Follow-Up

What if you don't get a response after reaching out by e-mail or phone? Sometimes, people grow embarrassed by how much time has passed since they responded to a call or e-mail and often feel too ashamed to get back in touch. So make it easy for them; break the ice and reestablish the lines of communication even though you weren't the person responsible for the breakdown.

This small concession on your part just might lead to big things down the road. By not taking offense to the long silence and reconnecting with the target, you are back in control of the relationship. You've gained points by taking the high road and will now undoubtedly hear back from your target. The guilt he carries can also be helpful in you gaining your target's business.

GROWING YOUR NETWORK

Look at all the people with whom you already have regular contact. Ask yourself whether this list of people has grown in the last month. If not, then it's time to put a bit more effort into expanding your network.

Think of all those various invitations that have landed on your desk. You know the sort of thing: this benefit, that gala, this bar mitzvah, that convention, this alumni gathering, and that conference. No doubt you have little interest in attending any of these functions, but these invitations are open doors in which to enter the great unknown and a chance to grow your network. When possible, you should always reply, "Yes, see you there." Why? You never know who you might meet. As the saying goes, the better part of success is just showing up.

Think about your most valuable customers and clients or your most influential contacts and how you first met them or became aware of their existence. Then trace it back even further and try to remember who connected you to that person? You might be amazed to learn just how much of your current business stems from having met a specific person at an event you originally dreaded attending.

I am a huge believer in the power of the unexpected meeting. A few years ago I was asked to fill in as host of a little-watched talk show. My duties would include interviewing a gentleman who worked for IT giant Oracle. I had little interest in the assignment and only agreed to host as a favor to the producer. I'm certainly glad I did. The gentleman was a delight and we hit it off so well during the taping of the show that he invited me to come and host one of Oracle's major corporate events. I've made a stream of valuable contacts, from many different organizations, which, to this day, form a solid 50 percent of my overall income thanks to this chance meeting. The contacts I made because of the Oracle connection are now spread across other companies, industries, and throughout the world. These contacts have introduced me to other individuals who in turn became contacts; and all have helped me generate a fabulous flow of business. There is no doubt in my mind that this single event on that one day—a meeting I nearly turned down—dramatically changed the direction of my career and life and has led me to great and continued success. New doors mean new success. So run, don't walk, when they stand open before you.

Hey, I'm Already Making Enough Money—Do I Need New Contacts?

You might not think you need any more friends or you're too busy with what's on your plate to worry about making new contacts or indeed that you now have over 1,200 Facebook friends!! I completely understand, but you must be careful, because success itself can often lead to your undoing.

The only thing that might be harder than becoming successful is staying successful. As time passes and you begin to enjoy the fruits of your labor, you might begin to think that you have it totally made. Loads of great clients, people calling you up all the time and business and cash flow pouring in might give you a false sense of security. It's at this point that you may start to become complacent and find yourself doing less marketing, making fewer exploratory calls, spending less time at new events, and no longer generating innovative ideas. You might believe that devoting all your time to your existing clients is the best way to continue to build your business.

This is always a mistake. Sure, it costs a lot more in the form of time and money to nurture and win a new client than it does to leverage an existing client, but eventually, without a stream of new clients using your services, you will become reliant on one or two big accounts, which is always a dangerous gamble. Business is a game of what have you done for me lately, so if one of these major customers ever becomes dissatisfied with you and ends your relationship, your bottom line will take a big hit without having other clients to offset this loss.

The flow of business that you enjoy during the good times was probably set up more than a year ago and it probably took that much time to mature the contact into a client, and even more time to turn that average client into a trusted client. Fast forward one year from today and your business flow will directly correlate with the amount of networking activity you're putting in at the present time. It's all a bit like gardening. You prepare the soil, plant your seeds and bulbs, and later in the year the flowers emerge and you see the products of your labor. Your contacts today are the pretty flowers of tomorrow. You need to constantly leverage and grow your network—keep planting the seeds so that later you can pick those flowers.

Business Card Alchemy—Turning Paper into Gold

If you are organized and you have categorized your new contacts into useful and useless, you are ahead of the game. But before you throw all those useless business cards into the trash, you should first try a bit of *e-mail matchmaking*.

That's right, those contacts may be of no value to you, but they could be gold to someone else. And if you hook up two contacts like some dating matchmaker, you'll build up big credits from both parties. Think for a minute about who you could connect with in your network, and send a matchmaker-type e-mail.

You know the sort of thing: "Hi, it suddenly occurred to me that you both have a lot in common and could probably do some great business together.... So, in true e-meeting style, Bob, top TV producer, allow me to introduce Sam, a vet who just happens to have a celebrity pet clinic. Let me know how it goes...."

Both of these people might be of little use to your business, but hey, to each other they just might a perfect business match. If they meet with success, your little act of thoughtfulness earns you some useful business payback credits. In fact, whether they successfully hook up or not, they'll both feel that they owe you something just for putting in a bit of effort to connect them. After all, not only did you think about them, but you also felt that they were both good enough at what they do for a living to suggest matching them up. There is no greater compliment you can pay either one of them.

Soft skills hugely affect the way you are perceived. When you bring together two distant contacts, you brand yourself as a connector of people, a business-minded networker, a friend, and someone who doesn't always put himself first. And this, my friend, is at the very heart of business seduction. Putting the concerns of others first is the key to winning new business and building trust with customers and clients. And from this trust flows limitless success.

Your Network—Your Salespeople

We all spend our lives exposed to advertising. We see or hear its messages on nearly every medium. We become enticed by its images as we are bombarded with its relentless impact. However, despite the Madison Avenue millions spent on advertising, it's often friends, family, and contacts who persuade us to buy a product. What I'm talking about is good old-fashioned word-of-mouth advertising. It's obvious why this is true. We trust the words of someone impartial far more than someone who stands to make some money from a particular transaction.

Let's take a television advertisement. This is the simplest example in the world: Scene: Middle-aged man in suit on car lot shouting in our direction, clutching granddaughter for emotional impact (nice). "Hi, I'm Brad Drake, and these are the finest cars your money can buy and this week we are having a sale to beat all sales. That's right . . ." and so forth.

When you watch this visual assault, do you drop everything and race down to the car dealership to buy as many of these quality, used vehicles as your wife's money will buy? Or do you mull over the idea of buying a car before completely deciding against it? Or do you scoff at this poor attempt to win you over and wonder what type of loser might actually fall for this trash?

Now imagine you're sitting down on a Saturday night with friends at a local restaurant and one of your closest acquaintances leans forward and says, "You won't believe how much money I saved on this car I just bought. Seriously, the dealer can't do his math. I bought such a great car for about two grand less than I should have done." Now you're most likely interested.

When you need a plumber to sort out a leak or a mechanic to fix your car, where do you go for recommendations? Do you thumb through the Yellow Pages or do you ask a friend who she last used in either case and whether that person was any good at his job? You trust the word of a friend or contact because you know they have nothing to gain by recommending someone to you. All they want to do is share a positive experience with you. And with your friend providing you valuable information, and you most likely having an equally enjoyable experience thanks to her recommendation, you'll more than likely want to pay her back at a later time. The circle of networking is ever expanding.

Your Network's Network

Here's where you call in all the favors you are owed. For example, imagine you run a small web design agency, and the people in your network—your existing clients—know how talented you are. It's time to make use of that goodwill.

People like to share new discoveries and welcome the chance to offer recommendations. So don't fret. As mentioned at the opening of the section, you must get over your fear of networking. Go ahead and make a call or send an e-mail and mention how you're entering your next phase of growth and ask your contacts if they know anyone in their own networks who could benefit from a cool, new-looking web site with innovative features. Then add a little incentive, letting them know that if they hook you up with someone new, you'll owe them a favor down the road. You'll be the best judge of just how far you can push this compensation, but it's important that you somehow convey that you are prepared to reward this special effort from them. The idea of payback is invaluable in a game of give and take.

SEDUCTION TAKEAWAYS

Do your research

If you are meeting people who might be of help to you, do your research. Read up on them and their industry, come brimming with facts that show you are already playing on their team.

Create the jealousy reaction

Whenever you can, tell a story and plant seeds that push your targets toward the jealousy reaction. Remember, your intention is to get them to *want* to work with you.

Let them go early

Time is precious—especially theirs! When the time is right, excuse yourself from a networking conversation, give them the gift of time, and smartly move on. They'll thank you for it.

It's alive!

Your network is a living and breathing entity. Nurture it with regular contact and feed it with new connections. Make it a monster and it'll pay dividends in the long run.

Social or online networking

Use it to supplement what you do offline—in other words, what you do in the real world. But don't forget to secure access to your more personal postings.

3Rs

This is the key to successful networking. Always obey the Radar, Recall, Reward rules, and you will not be forgotten. It is a surefire way to grow your valuable network.

You just never know

Take advantage of every single invitation or opportunity because you simply never know when that golden moment will arrive—so be ready and be there . . . all the time!

8

The Elevator Pitch—Going Up

Soft skills help immensely when you are deliberately networking, but they can also aid during more random and casual encounters in which you have even less time to make an impression. I like to call this the "elevator pitch."

The elevator pitch simply answers the question: "What do you do?" The idea being, that in the time it takes for a short elevator ride, you are able to explain to someone what you do, why you are good at it, the value and benefits of what you're offering, and why this stranger sharing an elevator with you should be interested in hiring you or at least referring you to people who might need your talents The elevator pitch puts a premium on soft skills because you have such a small window of opportunity to make an impression on a relative stranger about whom you know nothing. If ever you needed further evidence of the importance of drawing an instant connection with someone for the hope of personal gain, then you need to look no further.

Let's set aside that few people speak to each other when riding in an elevator. What you should actually be doing is seeing the time aboard an elevator—or in a stranger's company, however brief, as an excellent opportunity to advertise what it is you do.

Once inside an elevator, most of us generally stare ahead in morbid fascination at the glowing numbers on the panel wondering why it is taking so damn long to get up or down. Problems can often start even before the ride begins. Sometimes, once aboard, you may notice an individual racing for the door, ignoring the fact that another elevator will arrive shortly. This individual has spotted you and is making an appeal that you delay your take-off. Meanwhile, you create the illusion of fumbling for the door-open button, while actually furiously pressing the door-close button—a button that serves no true purpose, by the way—in hopes of getting on with your journey and reaching your destination, not to mention enjoying a moment of time alone.

With any luck, the doors will close in the face of the person running toward you, while you appear to try your best to open them, but then shrug your shoulders as he disappears from view. Ah well, you'll never see him again.

But, given that the gods tend to work against us, he sneaks in between the closing doors, and then strangely enough, this out-of-breath stranger starts talking to you. You need to be ready for such an interaction because, you simply never know, this guy might actually be able to help you achieve your goals, grow your business, or get a great job. He might also be of no help at all—that doesn't bother me because every interaction is an opportunity and you just never know. First impressions are lasting impressions, so begin this, or any other relationship, with the scales tipped in your favor. Get out in front, and stay out in front of the relationship by starting off on the right foot.

PREPARING YOUR PITCH

Creating an elevator pitch is a great exercise in not only determining the essential biographical information you should share with others upon first meeting them, but also in being able to share certain comments and ideas that may not directly suit the person in front of you. Cut out the irrelevant bits of data, linked normally to the process of what it is you do, and retain only the crucial elements that truly define who you are and what you are about. This is a key point in making yourself seem interesting and appealing and it also helps you in seducing an unsuspecting individual. You need to view the elevator pitch as another opportunity for you to brand and market yourself.

It's key to remember that you must never appear to be a smooth talking salesperson or political opportunist. Once people think you are playing a game, you lose any advantage. I am sure that you don't want this to be the way you are perceived, either—so make every effort to turn your pitch into a chatty, warm, and informed presentation. You want to come across as naturally friendly, using ostensibly casual conversation.

Your image should be comfortable, confident, and most of all, passionate—when talking about what you do. But what do you do?

You'd be surprised to learn just how many people are unable to effectively communicate what it is they actually do. Knowing you have this tool at the ready will boost your confidence and allow you to feel comfortable in random situations when you need to act quickly on your feet. Hone this pitch, prepare to use it when least expected, and no doubt it will lead to success at some point in time. If you ever read *Liar's Poker* by Michael Lewis, you'll recall that he got hired by Lehman Brothers because he charmed the wife of one of the firm's corporate bigwigs with whom he was seated at a fund raiser. This brief dinner conversation has led to life-changing experiences for Lewis. My advice to you: don't let opportunities like this pass you by.

FOLLOW THE RULES TO PERFECT YOUR ELEVATOR PITCH

Make your opening statement a shocker!

A good elevator pitch should be shaped like a pyramid—it starts at the apex with a short and snappy statement. Like a good TV commercial or movie trailer, the opening statement must grab attention. It should be enticing enough to make people actually *want* to listen to the rest of what you have to say.

Ideally, this initial comment should contain no more than six or seven words. The opening question might be as simple as, "So, what is it you do?" And your pitch will begin . . .

"I make dreams come true" (cosmetic surgeon) or "I create success" (financial director) or "I turn impossible visions into perfect buildings" (architect) or "I try to explain the world to the world" (journalist) or "I bring order to chaos" (IT developer).

You get the picture. Bold and arresting statements leave potential customer and client targets wanting to know more. Just remember, bold and arresting is quite different from over the top and ridiculous. Opening statements are like a calling card, so choose your words wisely. A statement like, "I make dreams come true," shows how you are in a position to help someone else. Whereas saying something like, "I'm a highly sought-after plastic surgeon," only shows how impressed you are with yourself. You should never be the one who awards yourself an accolade or testimonial.

THE PYRAMID APPROACH

After successfully deploying the opening salvo of your elevator pitch, you now need to begin building on the pyramid approach. After delivering your brief opening statement (the apex), you now need to broaden your pitch in two or three further stages enabling you to reach the base of the pyramid—which is the conclusion of your elevator pitch.

You can widen your approach and give your pitch a bit more definition by providing additional content that will hopefully trigger an "I need whatever this person is selling" reaction. This is the point when you begin convincing this individual that she not only wants to do business with you, but that she has to be in business with you.

Each statement should be a building block and complement the previous statement. As such, each stage will move you closer toward making a new contact, winning a new client, or gaining a new admirer.

For the sake of example, let's say you are a fitness trainer with valuable corporate and individual relationships. You also provide nutritional advice as well as training sessions. Likewise, you regularly write newsletters featuring tips and advice for your clients. Your business is doing well.

Let's Build a Pyramid . . .

Pyramid Level 1—Apex: Your opening statement: "I make bodies look good naked!"

Purpose: Intrigue your listener.

Intended response: *Sign me up!*

Pyramid Level 2: "I'm a high-level fitness trainer with a prestigious corporate clientele."

Purpose: Here's your slightly wider pyramid level—a great start to explaining the nature of what you do, what you offer, and the sort of people with whom you work.

Intended response: I still don't have all the facts but I find myself wanting to know more and learn how you got yourself into this specialized and presumably rewarding field.

Pyramid Level 3: "I work closely and personally with varied executives on their fitness, image, and health."

Purpose: You broaden your message further, defining several things you can offer. You paint yourself as more of a lifestyle coach than just a fitness trainer. You are ensuring the offer and appeal feels broad by using the term "varied executives." That's right. All are welcome. If you said, "financial executives," you would be limiting the sell by creating the image that either only financial executives come to you or that you offer services only to executives from the financial world. (Later on, however, you might reverse this approach by instantly guessing the background of the person in front of you and shifting the sell to his industry so that he feels he has just met someone who delivers services created specifically for people just like him.)

Intended response: *OK, I now know that you build close relationships with clients. They must value and trust you to let you in that close. I might be interested in health, fitness, or image. You have ensured that you mention them all as you spread your net a little wider.*

Pyramid Level 4: "Together we create an intense plan for exercise, diet, and lifestyle. I guide or push you to succeed at every turn. I'm not happy until you're happy."

Purpose: You've offered more details about what you do and a statement about your dedication to the job. Your pitch is focused and precise and yet gives you a wide base to support the apex of your pyramid.

Intended response: *You show you are a team player. You work with your client to create a blueprint for success. You are flexible enough to explain that in some instances you are not afraid to push people to achieve their objectives and at other times you'll use gentle guidance as your motivational tool of choice. You are confident in what you do and imply that your strategy works every time. I might not believe absolutely everything you say, but I'm going to hire you because I have faith that you deliver success.*

MATCHING THE PITCH TO THE PERSON

This is where the elevator pitch starts to deliver value for you. A regular pitch is simply a crafted statement designed to create interest. However, an instantly tailored pitch, using words and ideas to suit the perceived needs of the person you are targeting, can have a much more successful effect. In a matched or tailored pitch, you create the impression that what you do is *exactly* suited to the person in front of you. She concludes that you are utterly ideal for what she needs—and signs you up then and there (or within a short time, anyway!)

Using the fitness trainer example—if the person asking the question is already fit and strong, you would be better advised to refer to "maximizing performance" or "reaching the next level" rather than suggesting one get in shape. These phrases will resonate precisely with the fit and strong target, as it is probably what he has been thinking about. He will not have been considering starting work with a fitness trainer to try to get fit, as he already is fit—shape the sell to suit the buy!

And conversely, if the person is overweight or out of shape, you talk about how lifestyle changes in regard to diet and fitness can lead to a longer, happier, and healthier life. In this case, it's important to offer lots of enticement, promise, and potential so they see the benefits of committing to a long-range plan. Your pitch will be effective because it shows what you, as a trainer, can do for various clients. Your pitch is all about what you can do for your clients. It centers on the benefits she'll receive from working with you, not vice versa. You create the impression that you have nothing at stake here and you are only concerned with her best interests. This is the ultimate aim of soft skills.

The smartest pitches contain a core of facts that are surrounded by a flexible, dynamic set of sell ideas that can be altered to appeal in exactly the right way to the right person at the right time.

Sometimes it makes sense to jump straight in and reveal your pitch at the earliest opportunity—this goes back to learning to play your hunches. On other occasions, it is better to hold back a little, gather some essential data, and then reveal your pitch in a way that will directly appeal to the target. In situations such as this, your newly refined listening and watching skills come into play as your observations lead to your decision making.

VALUE AND BENEFITS VERSUS PROCESS

A lot of people can get hung up on pitching what they actually do to get the job done—I call this a "process pitch."

A process pitch simply lists the tasks you do to get your job done. It doesn't sell your value, only your day-to-day tasks. There is little within a process sell that would fire up the imaginations of a buyer or hirer.

Imagine you work in IT sales. It's your job to sell IT solutions to companies.

They ask, "So, what do you do?"

The process sell would look like this:

I spend my time researching potential clients to whom I can sell my company's software. I usually call them several times until I get an appointment. Then it's a case of going in there and trying to get them to buy as much as possible. My boss sets pretty high targets for me, so it's quite a task.

Yawn.

The Pyramid style, "Value and Benefits" sell totally focuses on what the advantages would be to the buyer of your products and services.

So, the question is, what do you do? The person asking is a CFO of a mid-sized engineering company.

Your Value and Benefits pitch:

I help my clients make more money.

Understanding the reality of my clients' industry objectives and challenges, I help them find and integrate state-of-the-art software.

Backed by a winning team, advanced industry knowledge, and years of experience, we match our client's business and financial needs with the best available software, services, and solutions.

This pitch is designed to appeal to the recipient in question. Looking at the pitch in order of play from the perspective of this potential client:

Who doesn't want to make more money?

I need all partners to understand my objectives.

Good, I am not being sold anything—you help me find it!

You have a winning team, advanced industry knowledge, and years of experience. Good—you grow my confidence with that background.

You'll match my needs with the best available software? That is what I am always looking for! I may not buy off you, but I am certainly interested in hearing more.

Let's use an encounter I had not too long ago as another example of choosing the best way to attack a situation.

On a recent vacation in Santa Barbara, I met a lawyer from a firm that I had never done any business with. I decided to wait for him to tell me all about his world before revealing mine. I soon learned that this guy had left his firm, only to return, and was now hopefully on the fast track to becoming a partner. I realized he was at a stage in his career when he had to ensure that his image, presentation, and communication skills were consistent with someone who would comfortably be selected as a new partner with this top-tier firm.

When it was time for me to say what I did, I simply used my standard pitch about helping organizations and individuals attain more success through smarter communication, networking, and soft skills, but added that I often worked with senior partners, newly promoted associates, and CEOs looking to improve their impact on shareholders, colleagues, and clients. That last statement was what struck a chord.

His response was exactly the result I desired. He said, "I must get your card before you leave." By putting my L-WAR skills to work, I was able to anticipate his silent concerns about being passed over for partnership and tailor my elevator pitch to exact specifications. I simultaneously demonstrated knowledge about his industry and understanding about his current personal concerns and objectives. Because of this subtle tweak, I found a new client.

Spend time on your elevator pitch. Think of it as a personal mantra. Then, like holding an ace up your sleeve in a card game, you'll be able to use your pitch to draw a winning hand. Sometimes all it takes is 30 seconds to change your life and lead you in new and wonderful directions. Never let these opportunities sail by. Always be prepared, because you just never know.

SEDUCTION TAKEAWAYS

When someone asks you what you do . . .

- Always have something ready to go—it's a free commercial, take advantage of the airtime. Saying, "Not much" or "It's a bit boring, really," will earn you no points at all.
- It's not a life story or the ultimate verbal autobiography. It's a 20-second window, so use the time well and remember that brevity is king.
- Make sure that whatever you say sells the *value and benefit* of what you do. Try not to get bogged down in *how* you do your job (the process), but do spend those valuable seconds explaining why what you do has value for them!
- Show passion. People like to see that you love what you do—it creates trust and confidence.
- Be smart and try to shape what you say to match the needs of the person in front of you. Using your powers of observation, try to guess what they will respond best to and say things that you know will check that box!
- At the end, exchange cards, smile, and try, if possible, to leave an anchor point at which you promise to reach out to her.

9

TECHNIQUETTE— THE ETIQUETTE OF TECHNOLOGY

Technology is a crutch we all lean on. From cell phones to e-mail to texting to the ubiquitous social networks—everyone feels the constant need to be in touch with home, the office, customers, and clients. But while all technological devices come with an owner's operating manual, they unfortunately don't come with a common-sense guide explaining "the do's and don'ts" of properly using these gadgets.

Everyone has a favorite device—for me, it's my Blackberry. So whether it's a Smartphone, iPhone, or Droid, we all clutch them with a death grip for fear if we lose the device we will lose our hold on life. There is an irrational fear that one missed phone call or one unreturned message will result in a customer fleeing for a competitor because they don't get the attention they feel they deserve or a boss screaming "You're fired" because he got bounced to voice mail. Just as these devices make our lives simpler, they inversely make them just as complicated, as we all wrestle with such behavior.

I have a serious affection (bordering on obsession) with gadgets of all kinds, so I am certainly not going to sing you a nostalgic song about the good old days of rotary phones and epistolary communication. I wholeheartedly advocate using these devices, but don't let them control your life. And when you do use them, use not only common sense but use consideration as well.

Here is a quick tutorial that won't cut off your technological lifeblood and will keep you from sabotaging any business and personal relationships with your technological dependence.

I LOVE YOU

I know what it feels like when my Blackberry receives a message—the gentle tone and pulsing light combine to confirm that I have friends, that people need me, and that my services are required. The effect is the same as a female siren on a tropical island drawing me in ... occupying my mind ... and my soul. Who can resist this unique and powerful call? The device is telling me that I am loved! The message reaffirms my existence as it tells me that someone, anyone, for that matter, needs my help.

Imagine you are sitting at lunch with a client, a colleague, or your boss and your Blackberry sparks to life. It takes great power, poise, and control not to look at the flashing screen. More than likely, you'll try to steal a quick glance (who is it?), if not try to read the message while your lunch partner is sneaking a look at the menu.

But be warned. When you do this, you are saying to the person sitting directly in front of you that at this moment your Blackberry is more worthy of your attention than she is. And now knowing one of the rules of soft skills is to make your target feel as if she is your main concern and sole point of focus, you can understand why this type of behavior is destructive. If you are happy to convey that message to the person with whom you are having an introductory business lunch, then by all means go ahead and consult your device. Just remember that impressions like this are hard to overcome and will tilt the scales against you and put the other person in control of the relationship, or worse, prevent the relationship from ever taking shape.

To capitalize on the seductive effects that soft skills can have on other people, you should make a knowing gesture of turning off, or at least silencing, your cell phone or smartphone at the beginning of every business meeting. This will definitely show that the person sitting across from you is your number one priority. Please, though, don't think putting it on vibrate is a good solution. There are few sounds more annoying and distracting than the constant humming these devices make when on vibrate.

BLUETOOTH

Bluetooth earpieces are a welcome method of heightening communication. These little devices are great when you are behind the wheel of your car or rushing through an airport while toting your luggage because they give you the freedom to continue to do business or stay in touch while your hands are otherwise occupied. However, I've started to see on a frighteningly large number of occasions that some people (always men, for some reason) elect to keep the earpiece in their ears during meetings and other face-to-face communication. Not only is this rude and unbecoming, it is also a fashion crime.

So, unless this Bluetooth has been surgically grafted into your ear, it should be removed before you talk to someone face to face. Some things are just that cut and dried. Should you choose not to remove your Bluetooth, this blatant act of disrespect will say more about you than any conversation you might have. This is Soft Skills 101. All your attention needs to be focused on the person sitting or standing in front of you. By wearing a Bluetooth device, you're saying loudly and clearly that any incoming calls are more important to you than the conversation at hand.

INSTANT MESSAGING (IM) OR TEXTING

Instant messaging is an accepted method of quick and casual communication. Within companies, it is an efficient way of posing questions, getting immediate responses, and instigating a friendly dialog. Still, certain rules should apply and certain considerations always kept in mind.

One of these considerations is that instant messaging is not a reliable method for tracking worthy conversations or decisions. If you are conducting business with a client or making important plans with friends or relatives, you should use e-mail so you can accurately keep all your records in a searchable, printable, and quotable digital file.

Likewise if you grow more reliant on instant messaging, you must resist the temptation to conduct communication like a 15-year-old text-messaging addict. "LOL, BOS, BRB[italic]" might well end up being your way of saying, "[italic]Laugh out loud, boss looking over shoulder and I'll be right back."

Unless this is the way your client communicates to you, this is no way for an adult to communicate or conduct business. There is nothing seductive about being immature. If anything, sending messages similar to the example in the preceding paragraph in any way, shape, or form may compromise any trust you had already established with the person on the receiving end of such a communiqué. Remember that everything that you choose to publish, be it e-mail, instant message, or social networking post, will all say something about you—all these communication moments either add to or subtract from your personal brand.

CORPORATE DATA BOMBS

If you want to infuriate somebody, send a stream of photos, graphics, a giant PowerPoint file, or a video that you either couldn't be bothered, or didn't know how, to compress for e-mail. This is known as sending a corporate data bomb. Drop one of these bombs on an unsuspecting client or colleague and not only will you blow up the recipient's inbox, you may even damage your relationship. So be courteous and compress any large files. It might be time consuming, but it will pay off on the back end. If your customer or client realizes you're willing to take the time to compress these files, she'll appreciate how you put a premium on her time and how you don't want her to waste it compressing files or navigating through a burdensome message.

E-MAIL ETIQUETTE

My guess is that if you're older than 30, you were never taught how to effectively and appropriately use e-mail. Odds are, e-mail etiquette was never a core requirement at whatever school you attended.

The problem is that a set of rules was never established upon the creation of e-mail. And to this day, there is no firm set of e-mail commandments. There is no right or wrong in the eyes of many. While everyone greatly appreciates the speed and effectiveness at which this medium allows us all to communicate, many of us abuse the casual nature of e-mail.

Some people are already calling for the end of e-mail, as they see the inexorable rise of inbox style messaging on other platforms like Facebook. Regardless of the electronic platform, though, we must all learn how to best use e-mail to make our lives, and the lives of our colleagues, customers, and clients better.

So What Are the Rules?

People must welcome your e-mails for you to be an effective soft skills communicator. Friends, clients, and colleagues must react to seeing your name in their inbox by opening your mail with enthusiasm, not dread. Those who receive your e-mail should anticipate something relevant, concise, interesting, appropriate, and of value. If your message doesn't elicit enthusiasm or curiosity, then why send it at all?

The following four rules will help you use e-mail as an effective means not only of communication, but of seduction.

Spelling and Grammar

The most important rule when sending an e-mail is that you must respect the longstanding rules of grammar and spelling. Never send a message littered with typos, misspellings, and grammatical errors. Yes, e-mail is instantaneous, but that doesn't mean you can hit the send button before proofreading. A general rule of thumb is to treat an e-mail message as you would a conventional letter. You would never put a letter in the mail unless you were sure all punctuation and grammar were correct; and this should be how you treat e-mail.

When you send a message, you reveal something about yourself. It's like saying, "Hey, check this out ... after years of education and experience this is how I write!" The question is: How do you want people to view you? Do you want them to see you as someone who is careless, or someone who takes pride in his work? I know the answer to this question. A well-written e-mail is further evidence of the thought and consideration you're willing to put into this potential relationship you're trying to jumpstart.

Before sending an e-mail, take the time to review the finished product. Correct the many inevitable errors—and there will be many—and only when satisfied that the message is thoughtful, coherent, and well-written should you hit the send button.

Words First, Address Second

Many people hastily write their message and click send, only then to think: "Aw, jeez, maybe I shouldn't have sent that much profanity. Oh well, too late now."

Adopt the following simple rule to avoid such a scenario. Write the content first, and once happy—and only when happy—address the message and hit "send." This rule will keep you from littering inboxes with incoherent ramblings. You never want to tip the scales of balance against you, and sending an ill-advised e-mail will do just that. You'll compromise whatever relationship you have with the person on the receiving end of that message.

Reply to All?

Sheer laziness and a decent amount of ass-covering has created a reply-to-all electronic society. Many feel it's a good thing when everyone can read what's on their mind. But this is not true—inboxes fill up quickly enough with vital information. Who wants to weed through an inbox filled with irrelevant minutiae?

Here is an example highlighting this point. Responding to a meeting request recently, a member of my client's team hit "reply to all" and sent this: "Hi, Karen, I thought I was going to be able to make this conference call and I still can, but I may be several minutes late as I have to take my mom for a few tests."

More than 30 people on the list now knew that this person's mother might be in need of surgery, hospitalization—or, indeed, further schooling. But quite clearly, only the meeting organizer needed to know that she would be late for the call.

We are a curious bunch, so this statement on its own was quite attention-grabbing for all the wrong reasons. How late would she be? What was the nature of these tests? Would she pass? Would she live? Was there no one else around who could drive the mom to the tests?

Believe it or not, it is possible to discover the impact on profitability of that particular "reply to all" through a simple calculation. Thirty people earning on average $80,000, is a total cost to the company of more than $2.4 million a year. Divided by the (approximately) 210 working days in the year, this costs the company, $11,428 every day—equal to approximately $27 per minute (seven worked hours across 60 minutes).

So that "reply to all," taking an average of a minute to open, read, laugh at, forward to others for entertainment value, and finally delete costs the firm $27. Happening many times a day and multiplied across a national economy in a year, that's literally millions of dollars lost on the reply-to-all function. In a world in which time is money, there is no further proof needed to demonstrate the frivolity of unnecessarily hitting "reply to all."

A less-is-more approach must also be adopted for the "CC" function. To copy in or not to copy in, that is the question. More often than not, additional people don't need to know—so before hitting "send" be sure that only those who need to see your message are in the loop.

By using discretion when sending an e-mail, you give the gift of time to those whom you spare from having to open unnecessary e-mails. And after all, time is the most precious commodity. Also, this selective approach to sending e-mail will guarantee that when someone sees your name pop up in her inbox, she'll know immediately that your message will be filled with relevant information and you'll be seen as someone of consequence.

If in a Rage, Save

How do you feel? Mad? Angry? Indignant?

If you feel any of these emotions and decide to vent in an e-mail, always force yourself to do just one thing. Save the message before sending it. Most of the time, you will choose later to edit this message or perhaps even delete it all together. Don't forget, you are the bigger person and your considered response—or lack of response—will have a far more positive impact than any knee-jerk reaction written in the heat of the moment. Don't let your feelings get the best of you. Remember, it's not personal, it's business. Take a deep breath and put yourself in the other person's shoes. No doubt he just needed to blow off some steam and the last thing he's looking for is an electronic war of words. Take the high road, and let time soothe the wounds. By doing so, you'll keep the relationship in good standing and keep open the possibility of future business dealings.

Demanding Notification

Do not demand a read-response to every single e-mail you send out. People get irritated when someone electronically demands to know if your e-mail has been read or not. "Adam has requested a confirmation that you read this e-mail. Would you like to respond?" No, I would not. Many people find this intrusive and unnecessary.

There is a smarter, more covert method of achieving the same objective, however, without causing any inconvenience or letting anyone know what you are up to.

One such solution comes from didtheyreadit.com. Once you sign up for the service (which is free), you are able to send e-mails through their servers. They arrive at your target's inbox with no sign of their hidden spy mechanism or the fact that they have been routed through these servers.

Once your e-mail is opened, you receive a confirmation e-mail from didtheyreadit.com. Better than that, the e-mail tells you how long your e-mail was read for, where (geographically) it was viewed, and how many times it was opened.

Too cynical and secretive for you? Don't do it, then. However, be aware that these secretive tables have already been turned on you. Plus, this covert measure doesn't make you seem needy or demanding. As far as the recipient knows, you're a cool customer. Remember back to the introduction: seduction is all about playing a role.

Brevity

E-mail is more convenient than picking up the phone because it allows you to briefly touch on points without having to endure the small talk. So, in keeping with the convenience factor, your e-mails should be concise and succinct. You don't want people to cringe when they see your name in their in-box or fear having to read through an incoherent and long-winded discourse. Every e-mail you send is a reflection of who you are and the value you have to offer, so don't squander an opportunity to impress. Whenever you have a chance to move the needle on the scale in your favor and gain control in any relationship, you have to capitalize on it. Who knows when the next chance will present itself.

Jokes

Your e-mails have a brand value. This value can rise as well as fall. If you start to forward every half-baked e-joke and monkey video that appears in your inbox, the brand value of your e-mails will drop as fast as the Dow Jones after a hike in unemployment.

Be very selective when deciding to forward jokes to your friends, colleagues, and clients. Ensure that when someone receives something like this from you that it's a rarity and something they will definitely find funny and just might instigate a conversation or exchange that builds even more trust in your relationship.

Check Your Privacy Settings

Whether using Facebook, MySpace, or some other social networking tool—you need to be fully in charge of the images and words that you post up there. There are many privacy settings to choose from and it is imperative that you select the right level of security so that all those crazy photos and comments that you add from the social side of your life can't be found on the business side of your life. The fact is, no matter what job or contract you are going for, people will google you. You will be searched! The question is, what will they find?

Take a moment out now to discover that for yourself. Go off and Bing or google your own name in quote marks—if there are millions of results, narrow it down by adding your company name or school name and see what others will find. If you are not happy, make some changes, delete some images, and feel stronger about protecting your personal and business online brand.

More on Brand Value

Each and every message you send has value and a purpose, so always try to maximize the impact. I try, wherever possible, to add a nugget of information, such as a link to a story, or a dash of gossip to ensure that when people read my e-mails they are getting two things—I want them to know they are receiving a message relevant to whatever our deal is, and they are also getting a message tailored specifically to them.

For example, I know one particular colleague who is a total airline obsessive. Every time I e-mail him, I attach a link to a cool new photo of the inside of the Airbus A380 or yet another prototype airplane. Another of my colleagues was having a few health issues, so in addition to some information he had requested on my coaching techniques, I sent him a newly published list of specialized doctors who may be of some use to him. These added gems help me improve the brand value of my messages. People know that, when they open my mail, they are going to get something extra. And this little something extra will no doubt leave a lasting impression as I strengthen our connection by showing I care about more than just our business relationship.

10

IMAGE

We all make split-second judgments. They are part of our everyday life. You probably think you have an idea about someone's income bracket, family background, and even his state of mind after walking past him in the street.

Your image, to a certain degree, helps determine your level of success—both through how others perceive you and, more importantly, how you perceive yourself. You obviously want to project an image of confidence and success. This is particularly true of business seduction and soft skills training. Positive first impressions are crucial in fostering trust and confidence in potential clients and customers or when interviewing for a desirable job. The slightest misstep in your appearance might well lead to not winning a big account or losing out on a promotion, whereas if you present yourself with style, poise, and control, you can rest assured you'll close just about any deal.

Decades of studies and statistical analysis show that people who present a positive image and are universally considered better looking do better in life. In *Why Men Lie and Women Cry*, authors Allan and Barbara Pease write about how "attractive men are paid twelve to fourteen percent more" than their ordinary-looking colleagues in the United States. A different study in Pennsylvania discovered that better-looking suspects received lighter sentences, and often no jail time at all, compared to unattractive defendants accused of the same crimes. And in Malcom Gladwell's *Outliers,* a study reveals that while only 14 percent of American males are over six feet tall, more than 60 percent of American male CEOs are also over six feet tall. Appearance counts!

Your image is not just how you look, it's also about how you appear, how you carry yourself. An air of confidence is ample compensation if you are not blessed with movie star looks. A strong presentation feeds confidence. Step out the door immaculately groomed and dressed in your best suit, and your confidence will be apparent to all who come in contact with you. Your confidence will inspire trust in others and lead them to actually want to do business with you. It truly is yet another part of the business seduction effort. But walk into a meeting with a stain on your shirt, your hair disheveled, or sweat pouring down your brow, and I can guarantee you customers and clients will think: *If this person can't take care of her appearance, how can I trust her to take care of our business?* Soft skills are all about trust and putting the other person at ease. Right or wrong, that trust can be built or broken, depending on many factors—including your appearance.

WHY DOES IMAGE MATTER?
You are always being judged.

People are constantly keeping score, even though there is no scoreboard or Jumbotron hanging from the sky. But what is the score? Well, you lose points for scruffy shoes, gain points for a Breitling watch, lose points for chipped nail polish, and gain points for a well-coordinated ensemble. Lose points, and customers and clients lose confidence—and you lose control of the relationship.

L'Oreal was right. You are worth it.

Image is everything. Despite all best intentions not to be superficial, image matters. And every time you add to that image, you win more points. Whether we agree with this or not—it really is how the world works—so polish up your image every chance you get.

First impressions last a lifetime.

Everything from your wardrobe choices to the way you style your hair to the manner in which you apply your makeup, to how accurately tied is your tie all show the outside world exactly whom they are dealing with. Be mindful of the choices you make because they will have a lasting impression. If people see you as the type of person who takes time and consideration when it comes to your image, they'll automatically believe you'll take the same consideration when their business interests are at stake.

Expect the unexpected.

Always dress to impress. Why take any chances? How can you be sure that on the day you decide to wear your oldest suit or fail to change torn stockings you won't bump into the person who might change the course of your life? As we discuss in the elevator pitch, sometimes all you have is a small window of opportunity to impress a stranger or a first-time contact. You will be judged before the first words ever come out of your mouth, so dress to impress.

PERSONAL GROOMING

Attention to detail is a key to success in business. This is especially true when it comes to personal grooming. After all, if you cannot take care of yourself, how on earth are you going to take care of your client? The perception you create is paramount to how you will be perceived by clients. It might seem silly, but if you can't be bothered to trim your nose hair or clean under your fingernails, why would someone think you would ever handle the little things that often determine success in business.

I was recently retained by the grooming giant Gillette to ensure that this message was not lost on their razor-buying customers. They carried out an exhaustive study of thousands of HR executives across the United States. Their findings were fascinating. Despite this world of political correctness, HR executives will still judge all applicants for a job on how they look, how well groomed they are, and the image they put across. In a competitive world in which equally qualified candidates are racing for the same job, contract, or pay increase—this study alone proves that a well-put-together image can tilt the scales in your favor. We read success, confidence, and trust into a well-put-together individual—take every chance to ensure that that advantage goes to you.

Clothes

Your wardrobe is one of the most visible and obvious statements of who you are. It is no longer acceptable to throw on any old thing because you don't have an important meeting that day, or to neglect your hair or makeup because you don't have a hot date. From this point forward consider such acts as "clothing crimes" and make a promise you'll never break that law again.

As attractive as casual Fridays may be to you, you need to ignore the temptation. Every day is the big meeting, the hot date, the golden opportunity. You naturally want to dress to match your style, but aim for the top end and enjoy the additional confidence that comes with a smart, sharp look.

Steal a Little Style

Whose public image do you most respect or admire? Whether it's Angelina Jolie or Brad Pitt, take note of what makes their style so distinctive and see what traits you can incorporate into your wardrobe. Do they have a certain trademark look or wear particular designers whose clothes always tend to complement them? Would that same look suit you?

Experiment a bit, but remember to dress to suit yourself, not as a poor imitation of someone else. The best impression you'll make is with an outfit that is suitable to your age, and is classically stylish as opposed to trendy. Timeless fashion choices are always a wise choice. A classic look shows you respect tradition and as such creates the impression you conduct business in an equally classy manner.

Designer Labels

Designer labels should be worn sparingly. Wearing an item from a designer's collection can highlight an outfit. It can serve as a personal trademark and distinguish you from everyone else wearing a dark suit or black cocktail dress.

If you are going to spend money like this, invest in looks that have staying power. If you must ditch an entire outfit after a single season, you didn't choose well. Select high quality looks that ooze style and the investment will pay off for two to three years, not two to three months.

Accessories

Any outfit, regardless of the cost, looks much sharper and more impressive when accompanied by a natty tie or designer handbag. And men, if you're wearing an expensive suit, don't wear a cheap belt or an inexpensive watch. When looking at men, studies have shown that people gravitate toward the suit, the watch, and the shoes.

Shoes are a Real Window to the Soul

A great outfit can be ruined by a scruffy pair of shoes. A good pair of shoes will last you two to three years and then, like an aging racehorse, they need to be put out to pasture. You will always be judged from the bottom up, so by investing in top-end shoes, you demonstrate that you recognize quality when you see it and appreciate the finer things in life. A wise shoe choice will reflect well on your business judgment and acumen. Look at your shoes as an investment and watch the dividends pay off.

And if you are to invest in those good shoes, please don't ruin the look with crazy multicolored or quirky socks that you may think are hilarious but everyone else thinks are a little sad!

Size Lies

Your choice of clothing must be comfortable enough for you to perform your daily tasks and yet tailored enough to show off any contours worth showing off. So, rather than squeezing into clothes two sizes too small or walking around in excessively baggy clothes, invest in smart, comfortable, tailored clothes that fit properly. If you are concerned about your weight, well-fitting clothes will actually make you look far slimmer than those that are too small. If you do shed the pounds in the future, then great, you can go and reward yourself with a new wardrobe. But in the meantime, you will still have been looking great and not undermining your professional image.

Being comfortable in your own skin is important in the business world. Colleagues and customers appreciate someone who is secure in who he is and not trying to be someone who he is not. Your wardrobe choices highlight this point. If people admire the way you dress, rather than ridicule you for trying to squeeze into ill-fitting pants or pull off wearing a short skirt, they'll feel more comfortable engaging you in conversation or perhaps entering into a long-term business relationship. The split-second decision they make upon coming into contact with you determines who controls the relationship from the outset, so your wardrobe needs to help you sell yourself in the best possible light.

Lucky Clothes

The psychology behind this lucky item of clothing is simple. In the past, you achieved something memorable while wearing this article of clothing, and from that day forward you have associated success with that outfit. What really happened, of course, was that the clothes you wore on that day made you feel confident, successful, and strong. You looked good, so you felt good, and as a result you exuded confidence.

This is a key point that follows all of the preceding advice on how you look. Whether you admit it to yourself or not, when you look good, the confidence that streams off you all day long has an almost tangible effect. People see it and feel it and, most importantly, they want to be associated with it. By dressing well, walking tall, staying fit, and appearing healthy, you are winning easy points that continue to tilt the all-important scales in your favor.

When you display confidence, people want to share your perceived success. Simply put, your confidence inspires their confidence.

THE DO'S AND DON'TS OF CLOTHING

- *Do* look stylish and up to date, but not ultra-fashionable.
- *Do* be aware of the "stop wearing by" date for any item—work on a two-season maximum.
- *Do* wear clothes that fit just right and accentuate your assets.
- *Do* dress for your (realistic) target image.
- *Do* care for your clothing.
- *Don't* try to be too sexy for work or too conservative for play.
- *Don't* neglect your personal grooming.
- *Don't* rush when making an important wardrobe choice.

Our Bodies

Most of us are dissatisfied with the way we look—don't worry, it's normal. Even people who look fabulous will hate something about their body. If you are one of the few people who look in the mirror and exclaim, "Wow, check me out," please skip this section and report immediately to the nearest modeling agency to launch your new career.

The good news is that with enough motivation, you can, of course, change the way you look—whether it's losing weight or toning up—through a sensible and balanced diet and regular exercise.

Lose Weight, Gain Confidence

Most people who lose weight share a similar story. They cite one particular day or moment that motivated them to change their lifestyle. In my case, it was seeing myself on a television monitor in the TV studio where I was working and having a co-presenter tell me that I looked a little . . . chubby. Not nice, but, unfortunately for me, quite accurate.

Propelled by those stinging remarks and my own harsh observations, I embarked on a period of eating less (which was very difficult because I absolutely love my food) and exercising a lot more (which was not difficult as I hadn't exercised at all up until that point). After six months, I was 35 pounds lighter, and my confidence was at an all-time high.

Although the weight coming off was a great result in its own right, what I hadn't fully anticipated was how much my business would improve as a result. Suddenly, new offers started coming in for speaking engagements and coaching work. It became clear to me that people were associating my weight loss with success, willpower, and motivation. They believed if I was able to achieve these weight-loss results, I could certainly help them achieve their business goals.

Body image may not be quite so important for someone who does not work in television or in the public eye. But, if you are carrying extra pounds, the biggest boost you can give your confidence, not to mention your health, is to find the motivation and incentive to lose the weight. Clients and customers will be inspired by your commitment and trust you'll bring that same level of dedication to any and all business dealings.

Healthy to Wealthy

People will react to a slimmer, fitter, and more-toned you in truly surprising ways. More people will want to know you. (Shallow? Probably! But it's reality.) A new level of confidence will undoubtedly be tangible. People will want to be associated with the positive vibes coming from you. You will meet with higher levels of success due directly to how you feel about yourself.

Walk Tall, Not Small

Shirley Bassey said it best many years ago: "The minute you walked in the joint, I could see you were a man of distinction." In any situation, the way that you enter a room and people's line of sight will say a lot about the person you are.

If you are a natural-born sloucher, odds are you will fail to make an impact on any room you enter. But good posture and confident body language will immediately draw attention and mark you out as someone other people will be interested in meeting.

In critical situations, most animals make themselves look as big and powerful as possible. In the animal kingdom, it's a case of puffing out your feathers, fur, face, or plumage to help you attract a mate or become leader of the pack. In our world, things are somewhat more subtle, but the same principles apply.

When you feel down or depressed, you are sure to take on a defeated or forlorn appearance. This normally manifests itself in slouching, accompanied by a sad face and downward-looking eyes. In the same way that we associate confidence with success, we also associate a lack of confidence with potential failure. So even if you're feeling down, ensure that your poise and body language is telling a totally different story. "Fake until you make," as they say. Business seduction, as discussed in the introduction, is about playing a role, so the part you must always play is that of the successful and happy person.

Be aware that it has to be credible and believable, and you certainly can't fake your way through your entire life. If you hit tough times, try not to show it when you are in public view.

Protect yourself from the judgment that will come and try not to seek out the sympathy that temporarily might make you feel better. Instead, try to think positively about how bad times always end and a sales rut always reverses and use that more positive thinking to fuel your appearance for that day.

Stand up straight, pull your tummy in, stick your chest out, and attempt to look as tall as you can. Flash a slight smile and appear like you are happy, certain, and secure. These actions make a tiny difference, but sometimes that's all you need to swing things in your favor. Business seduction boils down to tipping the scales in your favor. You do this by winning points by creating a favorable impression with everything from the clothes you wear to the shine on your shoes to how you style your hair.

The more points you win, the more you are in control of the relationship.

With so much at stake, it's imperative that you treat each business encounter like a first meeting. Never grow complacent or take a business relationship for granted. Treat each meeting like it is the most important of your career. Present yourself with style and confidence and you'll be met with trust in return. This trust will give you the upper hand in the relationship and is often the determining factor in success or failure when it comes to business. So it bears repeating: Looks do make the man (and woman).

11

SEDUCTION
MAINTENANCE

CONTINUING TO SEDUCE ... THE L-WAR
JOURNEY NEVER ENDS

None of what we have covered here is one-use-only.

None of it is a quick fix.

L-WAR is a way of business life. Yes, it is designed for your personal gain—but it also has the happy result of making other people feel good about their interaction with you. If, once you had your way with them, and you then disappeared—it would be as bad as the dating version of that cruel ditch!

Sometimes a client has no budget for you—or your boss cannot give you the pay raise you deserve. Is that game over? No. It's just the beginning. "No" might mean no. . . . But it also might mean "maybe in the future" or "keep trying" or "not now, but soon" or "no, not this, but maybe something else."

Building a trusted business relationship is a wonderful thing. This person will become your friend, will go to bat for you, and will throw business your way. In the beginning, though, you may see no results and you may find yourself wanting to abandon this new contact. Do not fall into that trap! Once that relationship is rolling—even if it is currently producing nothing for you—don't let it stop.

In many ways it's like filling up the gas tank in your car. You fill it up, you drive off, everything is great—but at some point the gas is going to run out and the car will no longer take you anywhere. Do you abandon it now? Or do you make the effort to drive to the gas station, whine about the price of gas, go out in the cold and fill it up again? Naturally, you fill it up. If you don't—if you give up on the whole refueling effort, the car won't have a chance to move again or serve you in any way.

The art of business seduction is the same thing.

And if I can continue the car analogy a little further—L-WAR is what keeps your car working for you. Hear an odd noise coming from the engine, you do something about it. See the fuel gauge dip or some red light flash—you deal with it. Winter is coming? You anticipate the frosty arrival by taking the car for a winter servicing before it's too late. See a hazard in the street; you react by slamming on the brakes. It's L-WAR on the road! If you had an amazing year with your car, you wouldn't stop your L-WAR activities in year two—you would continue. In fact, it never ends. Want to protect and preserve your car—you look after it.

Relationships in business and in our social life deserve the same care and attention. L-WAR in business allows you to care for your potential client, your boss, your team, your customer, your target.

English author and critic Samuel Johnson once said, "People need to be reminded more often than they need to be instructed." In fact, I start all my major keynote addresses with this quote.

However, in your ongoing business seduction you also need to continue reminding your targets, both won over and not yet won over, of why you are so great. Go back in the book to where I discussed the jealousy effect. Use great storytelling to plant those seeds of jealousy. I want people to conclude that they absolutely *need* you. You want them discovering, through your stories, that you are still successful and very much in demand. Once they hear that others use you, they will want to use you as well. No one likes to miss out on opportunities, and you need to keep on letting them know that you are great!

E-MAIL TIME TRAVEL

Seduction is a two way street—sometimes you actually need to give people permission to be seduced. This is when you need to ensure that you keep the e-mail wheel of fortune consistently spinning.

I noticed a fascinating dynamic when I reached out to people with whom I had not corresponded for quite some time. I nearly always got a reply, but more than that—I started getting messages saying things like, "Oh, I was just thinking of you—could you come in and help us on this?" or "Funny you should write, we were just putting together some ideas on an event which we would like your help on."

Was I really super-lucky with my timing? Was I simply reminding them of my existence? Or was it something else? I believe that it was a combination of both of those things, but also something else. People generally feel a little guilty when they don't communicate for a while and it puts them off reaching out. So, you need to be the big person here and remember that, in the end, being well-connected is a form of wealth. It may not be a monetary amount that you can instantly evaluate, but there is a tremendous value in your living and breathing network. So you owe it to yourself to keep it alive by always staying in touch. On the upside, you'll never know what amazing opportunities will arise from a random reach-out. And if nothing else happens, you still have a contact who may or may not be of use at some point in the future.

Back through time!

Here's how I deal with it. Every month or so, I hit the down arrow on my inbox. Like a little version of a time machine, I watch the dates zipping past and I keep going until I get about four or five months back in time. Then I stop. At this point, I start slowly going through e-mails of that time. Naturally, there are many messages that were pertinent then but have no meaning now, but suddenly I'll see a name. Someone I met at an event—someone who had me come in and do some communication coaching, someone who had asked about my availability but then disappeared. These are the people I now reach out to.

I'll send a message like this:

Hi Tom,

Haven't heard from you in a while so I thought I would reach out and say hi.

(I do a bit of research and see that their company just took on a new leader)

I saw that you guys have taken on a new CEO—hope that's going well—does it change your role or responsibilities at all?

(In his last message he had mentioned that he was attending an event in Orlando during this actual week)

I think you may be in Orlando at the moment—so just for fun, I found this cool web site with non-Disney restaurants and cool places to go visit—enjoy!

Let's stay in touch and meet up soon,

All the best,
M

Now this is a form of the 3Rs of networking—but with someone who has disappeared from the radar. It may or may not get a response—but as it says on the back of my business card, "If you don't ask, you don't get." What am I asking for here? Not much, just a reply. Why do I deserve one? Well, I sent him that cool web site and I went out of my way to reach out to say "Hi."

Nothing is guaranteed, but this is a nice way to spin the e-mail wheel of fortune and see where it lands.

The Only Thing Harder Than Getting to the Top . . . Is Staying There

Don't forget that people are judging you the whole time, so make sure your e-mails, blogs, posts, FB updates, tweets, and so forth portray you how you want to be seen.

It's easy to become a little complacent with our written communications and messages. Life becomes so busy and trying that we end up rushing and racing to make ourselves heard, to get messages across and to respond to people's demands. However, like a movie star in front of the paparazzi, we are always on. People are always watching and judging us, and worse still, there are young, ambitious individuals ready to take our crowns in a flash.

As distressing as this may sound—don't let go. Never take your foot off the gas, or your hands off the reins, or your eye off the ball! One way to do this is to always check through your outgoing messages before you click "send." All electronic messaging, whether a post, a tweet, an IM, or e-mail lasts forever. Sure, you may try to delete something, but you know it exists out there somewhere.

MANAGING EXPECTATIONS—SCOTTY STYLE

Two *Star Trek* analogies for you now. I must confess I am a Trekkie. I don't dress up like Captains Picard or Kirk or a Klingon, but I love those shows and movies. I think I get lost in the fantasy—in the escapism and a view of the future.

Scotty, from the original series, used to do something very clever when dealing with the original Captain Kirk. There would be some disaster requiring an escape of sorts. Naturally, however, the warp engine would always be damaged and in need of repair. In a slow zoom of a shot, Kirk would radio down to engineering and say, "Scotty, I need those engines now!" Scotty would then beautifully manage expectations. He would radio back, "Captain, I need two hours!" and a time line was set.

Little did Kirk know that Scotty needed only one hour. Even if his repair work ran over by 30 minutes, he would still be able to radio back to Kirk that the engines were ready early and they could escape at warp speed off into the distance of deep space. By taking this approach, Scotty always delighted his captain by surprising him on the upside. Can you imagine if he had taken the opposite approach and had promised to do the work in 30 minutes? Then an hour late, finally report them ready? Grim faces all around on that bridge, I suspect.

There is no reason why we too can't take a leaf out of this book. Whenever you are delivering a project or running a meeting, set expectations that you can always beat. You have a meeting planned that should take around an hour? Tell everyone it's a 90-minute meeting. Even if you run over the hour by 15 minutes, you still look like quite the hero when you release everyone early and give them all an unexpected, but warmly welcomed, gift of time.

The airlines play that trick on us. We all know that the flight time from London Heathrow to Paris CDG is only about 40 minutes—but in the timetable it is listed as a 90-minute flight. That way they always land early.

GIVE THEM WHAT THEY WANT

Don't be afraid to keep reinventing yourself. The original *Star Trek* series back in the 1960s ran its course on television before reaching the big screen in feature films. Next up came the next generation of television show—Patrick Stewart as Captain Picard, *Deep Space Nine*, then *Voyager* with female Captain Janeway, after which Captain Archer took us back to before Kirk and finally (for the time being) the reimagining of young Kirk and Spock in the hit 2009 movie.

One product, many variations. The team behind the franchise sees a changing public with different needs and expectations and they create something that they hope meets the demand. We as individuals must keep on reinventing ourselves. Sometimes a subtle shift, other times a total change of direction. The golden rule, though, is this—give them what they want.

Be smart enough to use your L-WAR skills to read the reality of your business landscape and keep on delivering the version of yourself—your own personal and business brand that you can tell will be in demand. Being switched on like this will always keep you steps ahead of your competitors. People fear change and there is little more comfortable than keeping everything the same—but that's how people fall behind and lose the lead! Take time to think:

- How can I do this differently?
- Who would I lose and who would I win?
- Do I need to update my look/my sell/my site?
- What excites people today? Am I in that field?
- Step by step or wholesale reinvention? How fast should I move?

BE NICE ON THE WAY UP . . .

When I was involved in television, there was an old saying that used to do the rounds. It was presumably coined as a result of how fast you can go from zero to hero in that industry. One day you are a researcher, the next day you are doing the weather, the next week you are live on the set interviewing a prime minister or president. When those lucky chosen ones were enjoying their dizzying ascent to the top, wise friends would take them to one side and say, "Be nice to people on the way up, so that they'll be nice to you on your way down." A little cruel or very smart?

To me, these were wise words. On my business card, I summarize it differently. I simply write: Never burn bridges.

But the thinking is exactly the same. When you meet with success (and you will), people will do anything for you, and you can become drunk on the sensation of power and control. It becomes easier to dismiss people who no longer seem relevant. You may stop returning as many calls and e-mails because there simply isn't the time. If you are self-employed and your daily fee or charge-out rate rises dramatically, you will now feel the need to get rid of those low-value clients—leave them all behind in the wake of your sparkling dust . . . .

But beware. The rise to the top is an uneven and tricky climb. There will be good times and there will be bad times. Be optimistic, be positive, but always temper your enthusiasm with a dose of reality. If things do go bad for awhile, you will need those low-value clients, those old friends, those whom you so easily dismissed.

L-WAR works down just as much as it works up. Take care of people so they'll take care of you. . . . Be nice on the way up!

L-WAR—A LONG-TERM INVESTMENT

If you have stuck to this 30-day plan, it has, with luck, already positively altered the way you approach all business communications scenarios—whether sales, negotiation, promotion, or leadership.

Much as we would like it all to pay off immediately, it is sometimes just a case of planting a few seeds and going away. They say that a healthy diet—one that keeps the weight off—is a lifelong commitment, a revolution in the way that you select and eat food. Business seduction is the same. You cannot seduce for a month and then return to your old ways and hope for the success to continue. This new approach is one that will pay dividends on an ongoing basis as long as you stick to the ideals within it.

You are a proactive monitoring station—you now see more than you have ever seen. You listen and you hear far deeper than in the past. Your mind now constantly sets up potential scenarios that could follow any conversation; your actions smoothly shift to suit the potential outcomes of your discussions, meetings, and chance encounters. You are ready with a conversational elevator pitch that adapts instantly to the person listening. You are now a connector of people, you are in touch, you are seen as an expert. You are perceived as confident, in control, interested, enthusiastic, and capable.

You are always on—you never stop listening, watching, anticipating, and reacting.

The L-WAR is yours to win!

INDEX